First World War
and Army of Occupation
War Diary
France, Belgium and Germany

15 DIVISION
44 Infantry Brigade
Seaforth Highlanders (Ross-shire Buffs, the Duke of Albany's)
8th Battalion
1 August 1916 - 30 September 1916

WO95/1939/3

The Naval & Military Press Ltd
www.nmarchive.com
Published in association with The National Archives

Published by

The Naval & Military Press Ltd

Unit 10 Ridgewood Industrial Park,

Uckfield, East Sussex,

TN22 5QE England

Tel: +44 (0) 1825 749494

www.naval-military-press.com

www.nmarchive.com

This diary has been reprinted in facsimile from the original. Any imperfections are inevitably reproduced and the quality may fall short of modern type and cartographic standards.

© **Crown Copyright**
Images reproduced by permission of The National Archives, London, England, 2015.

Contents

Document type	Place/Title	Date From	Date To
Heading	War Diary. of the 8th (Service) Battalion Seaforth Highlanders. From 1st August 1916 To 31st August 1916 Volume XIV		
Heading	44th Brigade. 15th Division 1/8th Battalion Seaforth Highlanders. August 1916 Appendices 1 to 51		
War Diary	Naours.	01/08/1916	04/08/1916
War Diary	Mirvaux	04/08/1916	05/08/1916
War Diary	La Houssoye.	05/08/1916	08/08/1916
War Diary	Albert	08/08/1916	11/08/1916
War Diary	N.29.d. Central Albert Combined Sheet 1/40000.	12/08/1916	12/08/1916
War Diary	A.29.d. Central.	13/08/1916	13/08/1916
War Diary	Scots Redoubt.	14/08/1916	15/08/1916
War Diary	Scots Redoubt Peake Wood.	16/08/1916	16/08/1916
War Diary	Contal Maison	17/08/1916	17/08/1916
War Diary	Gourlay Trench.	17/08/1916	20/08/1916
War Diary	Scots Redoubt.	20/08/1916	21/08/1916
War Diary	Peake Wood.	22/08/1916	23/08/1916
War Diary	Contal Maison	24/08/1916	25/08/1916
War Diary	Gourlay Trench	26/08/1916	28/08/1916
War Diary	Scots Redoubt	28/08/1916	30/08/1916
War Diary	N. Albert M. 29 D 8.4.	31/08/1916	31/08/1916
Miscellaneous	44th Brigade B.M. 671.	01/08/1916	01/08/1916
Operation(al) Order(s)	Operation Order No 10 by Lieut. Col. N.A. Thomson, D.S.O. Commdg 8th Bn. Seaforth Highlanders.	03/08/1916	03/08/1916
Miscellaneous	March Table to accompany 44th Infantry Brigade Operation Order No. 71.	03/08/1916	03/08/1916
Operation(al) Order(s)	Operation Order No. 11 by Lieut. Col. N.A. Thomson D.S.O.-Commdg. 8th Bn. Seaforth Highlanders	04/08/1916	04/08/1916
Miscellaneous	March Table to accompany 44th Infantry Brigade Operation Order No. 72	04/08/1916	04/08/1916
Miscellaneous	44th Bde. B.M. 28.	05/08/1916	05/08/1916
Operation(al) Order(s)	Operation Order No. 12. By Lieut Col. N.A. Thomson D.S.O. Commanding. 8th (S) Battalion Seaforth Highlanders.	07/08/1916	07/08/1916
Miscellaneous	March Table to accompany 11th Infantry Brigade Operation Order No. 73.	06/08/1916	06/08/1916
Miscellaneous	83 Seaforth Hrs. D./244.		
Miscellaneous	8th (S) Bn. Seaforth Hrs.-D./243	10/08/1916	10/08/1916
Miscellaneous	O.C. All Bombardiers	12/08/1916	12/08/1916
Miscellaneous	44th Brigade B.M. 743.	11/08/1916	11/08/1916
Miscellaneous	15th Division Special Operation Map No. 1. Martinpuich		
Miscellaneous	O.C. All Coys.	11/08/1916	11/08/1916
Miscellaneous	A Form. Messages And Signals.		
Operation(al) Order(s)	Operation Order. No 13 by. Lieut. Col. N.A. Thomson, D.S.O. Commdg. 8th (S) Battn. Seaforth Highlanders	13/08/1916	13/08/1916
Operation(al) Order(s)	44th Infantry Brigade Operation Order No. 74	13/08/1916	13/08/1916
Miscellaneous	Relief Table to accompany 44th Infantry Brigade Operation Order No. 74		
Miscellaneous	A Form. Messages And Signals.		

Miscellaneous	Officers Commanding.	12/08/1916	12/08/1916
Miscellaneous	C Form (Original). Messages And Signals.		
Operation(al) Order(s)	Operation Order No 14 by. Lieut. Col. N.A. Thomson. D.S.O. Comdg 8th Bn. Seaforth Highlanders.	15/08/1916	15/08/1916
Miscellaneous	44th Brigade. B.M. 800.	15/08/1916	15/08/1916
Miscellaneous	C Form (Original). Messages And Signals.		
Operation(al) Order(s)	44th Infantry Brigade Operation Order No. 75.	16/08/1916	16/08/1916
Map	15th Division Map No. 3.		
Operation(al) Order(s)	Operation Order No 15 by Lieut. Col. N.A. Thomson. D.S.O. Commdg 8th (S) Bn Seaforth Highlanders	16/08/1916	16/08/1916
Miscellaneous	A Form. Messages And Signals.		
Operation(al) Order(s)	44th Infantry Brigade Operation Order No. 77	17/08/1916	17/08/1916
Operation(al) Order(s)	Operation Order No. 16 by Lieut. Col. N.A. Thomson Comdg 8/Sea. Highrs	17/08/1916	17/08/1916
Miscellaneous	A Form. Messages And Signals.		
Miscellaneous	OC. All Companies	18/08/1916	18/08/1916
Miscellaneous	A Form. Messages And Signals.		
Diagram etc	Plan Of Attack On Switch Elbow.		
Miscellaneous	Report on B Coy 8th Seaforth Highlanders Operations On August 17 1916.	21/08/1916	21/08/1916
Miscellaneous	Addendum No. 2 to 44th Infantry Brigade Operation Order No. 76.	17/08/1916	17/08/1916
Miscellaneous	Addendum No. 1 to 44th Inf. Bde. Operation Order No. 76.	17/08/1916	17/08/1916
Operation(al) Order(s)	44th Infantry Brigade Operation Order No. 76.	17/08/1916	17/08/1916
Miscellaneous	A Form. Messages And Signals.		
Miscellaneous	44th. Inf. Bde.	18/08/1916	18/08/1916
Miscellaneous	C Form (Original). Messages And Signals.		
Miscellaneous	A Form. Messages And Signals.		
Operation(al) Order(s)	Operation Order 16 By Lt. Col. N.A. Thomson. D.S.O. Comdg 8th Battn Seaforth Highrs	19/08/1916	19/08/1916
Operation(al) Order(s)	44th Infantry Brigade Operation Order No. 76	19/08/1916	19/08/1916
Operation(al) Order(s)	Operation Order No. 17. by Lieut. Col. N.A. Thomson, D.S.O. Commdg. 8th (S) Battn. Seaforth Highrs.	21/08/1916	21/08/1916
Operation(al) Order(s)	44th Infantry Brigade Operation Order No. 79.	21/08/1916	21/08/1916
Miscellaneous	44th Bde B.M. 18/S	23/08/1916	23/08/1916
Operation(al) Order(s)	Operation Order No. 18 by Lieut. Col. N.A. Thomson, D.S.O. Commdg. 8th Seaforth Highlanders	23/08/1916	23/08/1916
Operation(al) Order(s)	44th Infantry Brigade Operation Order No. 80.	23/08/1916	23/08/1916
Miscellaneous	All Units 44th Inf. Bde. Warning Order.	24/08/1916	24/08/1916
Miscellaneous	A Form. Messages And Signals.		
Miscellaneous	15th Div. No. 114/2 G.b.	25/08/1916	25/08/1916
Miscellaneous	A Form. Messages And Signals.		
Map	8.S.H.		
Operation(al) Order(s)	44th Infantry Brigade Operation Order No. 81.	26/08/1916	26/08/1916
Miscellaneous	A Form. Messages And Signals.		
Map	Left Coy "D"		
Miscellaneous	Defence Scheme by Lieut. Col. N.A. Thomson, D.S.O. Commdg. 8th Bn Seaforth Highlanders	27/08/1918	27/08/1918
Miscellaneous	Bomb & S.A.A. Stores Appendix "A"		
Miscellaneous	Patrols.		
Miscellaneous	A Form. Messages And Signals.		
Miscellaneous	Intelligence Summary to 7:30 a.m.	28/08/1916	28/08/1916
Operation(al) Order(s)	44th Infantry Brigade Operation Order No. 82.	27/08/1916	27/08/1916
Operation(al) Order(s)	Operation Order No 19 by Lieut. Col. N.A. Thomson, D.S.O. Comdg 8th (S) Battn. Seaforth Highlanders	27/08/1916	27/08/1916

Type	Description	Date From	Date To
Operation(al) Order(s)	44th Infantry Brigade Operation Order No. 83	28/08/1916	28/08/1916
Operation(al) Order(s)	Operation Order No. 20 by. Lieut. Col. N.A. Thomson, D.S.O. Commdg. 8th (S) Battalion Seaforth Highlanders	29/08/1916	29/08/1916
Miscellaneous	Addendum No. 1 to 44th Infantry Brigade Operation Order No. 84.	28/08/1916	28/08/1916
Operation(al) Order(s)	44th Infantry Brigade Operation Order No. 84.	28/08/1916	28/08/1916
Miscellaneous	Table to accompany 44th Infantry Brigade Operation Order No. 84	28/08/1916	28/08/1916
Miscellaneous	All Units 44th I.B. Warning Order.	29/08/1916	29/08/1916
Miscellaneous	8th (Service) Battalion. Seaforth Highlanders.	01/08/1916	01/08/1916
Heading	War Diary Of 8th (Service) Battalion Seaforth Highlanders. From 1st September 1916 to 30th September 1916. Vol 10		
War Diary	N. Albert.	01/09/1916	01/09/1916
War Diary	N.29.d.8.4.	01/09/1916	04/09/1916
War Diary	Scots Redoubt.	05/09/1916	05/09/1916
War Diary	O.G.I.	06/09/1916	07/09/1916
War Diary	Quarry.	07/09/1916	09/09/1916
War Diary	OG1 & OG2	10/09/1916	12/09/1916
War Diary	Bivouac. X.26.b.	13/09/1916	13/09/1916
War Diary	X.26.b.	14/09/1916	14/09/1916
War Diary	Peake Wood.	15/09/1916	16/09/1916
War Diary	Contalmaison.	17/09/1916	17/09/1916
War Diary	Martin Puich	17/09/1916	18/09/1916
War Diary	Albert.	19/09/1916	19/09/1916
War Diary	Lavieville	19/09/1916	20/09/1916
War Diary	Franvillers	20/09/1916	30/09/1916
Operation(al) Order(s)	Operation Order No 21 by Lieut. Col. N.A. Thomson D.S.O. Commdg. 8th (S) Battn. Seaforth Highlanders.	03/09/1916	03/09/1916
Operation(al) Order(s)	Operation Order No. 22. By Lieut. Col. N.A. Thomson. D.S.O. Commdg. 8th Battn. Seaforth Highlrs	04/09/1916	04/09/1916
Operation(al) Order(s)	Operation Order No. 23. By Lieut. Col. N.A. Thomson. D.S.O. Commdg. 8th Battn. Seaforth Highlrs	07/09/1916	07/09/1916
Miscellaneous		07/09/1916	07/09/1916
Miscellaneous	Officers Commanding. All Companies	02/09/1916	02/09/1916
Miscellaneous	44.I.B. B.M. 154.	07/09/1916	07/09/1916
Miscellaneous	O.C. All Companies. Lewis Gun Officer.	07/09/1916	07/09/1916
Miscellaneous	44th Brigade B.M. 31.	11/09/1916	11/09/1916
Miscellaneous	Work for Night 12th/13th Septr.	12/09/1916	12/09/1916
Operation(al) Order(s)	Operation Order No. 25 by Lieut. Col. N.A. Thomson D.S.O. Commdg. 8th Battn Seaforth Highlrs	09/09/1916	09/09/1916
Operation(al) Order(s)	Operation Order No. 25 by Lieut. Col. N.A. Thomson D.S.O. Commdg. 8th Battn Seaforth Highlrs	12/09/1916	12/09/1916
Miscellaneous	All Units 44th Inf. Bde.	08/09/1916	08/09/1916
Operation(al) Order(s)	Operation Order No. 24. by. Lieut Col N.A. Thomson D.S.O. Commdg. 8th Seaforth Highlanders.	08/09/1916	08/09/1916
Miscellaneous	44th Brigade. B.M. 231.	13/09/1916	13/09/1916
Map	15th Div. Map No 6		
Miscellaneous	Proposed Relief Programme.	06/09/1916	06/09/1916
Map	Secret		
Map	15th Div. Map No 6B		
Map	15th Division Map No. 9		
Operation(al) Order(s)	Operation Order No 27. by. Lieut. Col. N.A. Thomson D.S.O. Commanding 8th Battn Seaforth Highlanders	14/09/1916	14/09/1916
Miscellaneous	15th Division Summary of Operations.	15/09/1916	15/09/1916

Type	Description	Date	Date
Operation(al) Order(s)	44th Infantry Brigade Operation Order No. 92.	12/09/1916	12/09/1916
Miscellaneous	Table to accompany 44th Infantry Brigade Operation Order No. 92.	12/09/1916	12/09/1916
Map	13th Div. Map. No. 8		
Operation(al) Order(s)	44th Infantry Brigade Operation Order No. 93	14/09/1916	14/09/1916
Miscellaneous	44th Brigade B.M. 197.	10/09/1916	10/09/1916
Operation(al) Order(s)	Operation Order No. 29. by Lieut. Col. N.A Thomson D.S.O. Commdg. 8th Battn Seaforth Highlanders	17/09/1916	17/09/1916
Operation(al) Order(s)	Operation Order No. 32. by Lieut. Col. N.A Thomson D.S.O. Commdg. 8th Battn Seaforth Highlanders	19/09/1916	19/09/1916
Miscellaneous	All Units 44th Inf. Bde. Warning Order.	03/09/1916	03/09/1916
Diagram etc	Issued With 15th Division Letter No. 108/I.G		
Miscellaneous	Work Report to 6 a.m. 8th Sept 1916	08/09/1916	08/09/1916
Miscellaneous	Intelligence Report to 8 a.m. 8/9/16	08/09/1916	08/09/1916
Miscellaneous	Work Report to 6 a.m. 9/9/16	09/09/1916	09/09/1916
Miscellaneous	Intelligence Summary to 9 a.m. 9th Sept 1916	09/09/1916	09/09/1916
Miscellaneous	All Units 44th Inf Bde.	01/09/1916	01/09/1916
Miscellaneous	44th Brigade. B.M. 102.	02/09/1916	02/09/1916
Miscellaneous	Correction No 2 to 44th Inf. Bde. O.O. No 89	08/09/1916	08/09/1916
Miscellaneous	8th Seaforth Hdrs. Correction No. 1. To 44. I.B. O.O. No 89.	08/09/1916	08/09/1916
Miscellaneous	44th Brigade B.M. 153	07/09/1916	07/09/1916
Miscellaneous	Correction No 1 to Operation Order No 25	09/09/1916	09/09/1916
Miscellaneous	Intelligence Report to 7.30 a.m.	10/09/1916	10/09/1916
Map			
Diagram etc	Trenches to be dup.		
Miscellaneous			
Operation(al) Order(s)	Operation Order No 28. by. Lieut. Colonel N.A. Thomson D.S.O. Commdg 8th Seaforth Highlanders	16/09/1916	16/09/1916
Miscellaneous	A Form Messages And Signals.		
Miscellaneous	There Already Constructed in M 26 C.	17/09/1916	17/09/1916
Miscellaneous	Note	17/09/1916	17/09/1916
Miscellaneous	O.C. "A" & "C" Companies	18/09/1916	18/09/1916
Miscellaneous	O.C. "A" Coy	18/09/1916	18/09/1916
Miscellaneous	C Form (Original). Messages And Signals.		
Miscellaneous	The 9th Black Watch. 8th Seaforth		
Operation(al) Order(s)	Operation Order No 31 by Lieut Col N.A. Thomson DSO Commdg 8th Seaforth Highlrs	19/09/1916	19/09/1916
Miscellaneous	O.C. All Companies. Lewis Gun Officer. Pioneer Officer. 44th I.B. (for information)	21/09/1916	21/09/1916
Miscellaneous	O.C. All Coys. Lewis Gun Officer. Pioneer Officer. Quartermaster (for information)	21/09/1916	21/09/1916
Miscellaneous	O.C. All Coys. Lewis Gun Officer. Pioneer Officer. Quartermaster (for information)	22/09/1916	22/09/1916
Miscellaneous	O.C. All Coys. Lewis Gun Officer. Pioneer Officer. Quartermaster (for information)	24/09/1916	24/09/1916
Miscellaneous	O.C. All Coys. Lewis Gun Officer. Pioneer Officer.	25/09/1916	25/09/1916
Miscellaneous	O.C., All Coys. Lewis Gun Officer. Transport Officer. Pioneer Officer.	26/09/1916	26/09/1916
Miscellaneous	O.C. All Coys. Lewis Gun Officer. Pioneer Officer.	27/09/1916	27/09/1916
Miscellaneous	O.C. All Coys.	27/09/1916	27/09/1916
Miscellaneous	O.C. All Coys. A/13.	28/09/1916	28/09/1916
Miscellaneous	O.C. All Coys. Quartermasters.	29/09/1916	29/09/1916
Miscellaneous	O.C. All Coys. Lewis Gun Officer. Pioneer Officer. 44th I. Bde (for information)	29/09/1916	29/09/1916
Miscellaneous	8th (Service) Battalion Seaforth Highlanders.	30/09/1916	30/09/1916

Miscellaneous	Reinforcements for the month of September, 1916. Officers.	30/09/1916	30/09/1916
Operation(al) Order(s)	44th Infantry Brigade Operation Order No. 85.	03/09/1916	03/09/1916
Operation(al) Order(s)	44th Infantry Brigade Operation Order No. 86	04/09/1916	04/09/1916
Miscellaneous	Relief Table To Accompany 44th Infantry Brigade Operation Order No. 86	04/09/1916	04/09/1916
Miscellaneous	44th Brigade B.M. 124.	05/09/1916	05/09/1916
Miscellaneous	A Form. Messages And Signals.		
Operation(al) Order(s)	44th Infantry Brigade Operation Order No. 87.	07/09/1916	07/09/1916
Operation(al) Order(s)	44th Infantry Brigade Operation Order No. 88	07/09/1916	07/09/1916
Map	Issued With. 44.I.B.O.O. No 88		
Miscellaneous	A Form. Messages And Signals.		
Operation(al) Order(s)	44th Infantry Brigade Operation Order No. 89.	08/09/1916	08/09/1916
Miscellaneous	44th Brigade B.M. 190	09/09/1916	09/09/1916
Operation(al) Order(s)	44th Infantry Brigade Operation Order No. 90.	08/09/1916	08/09/1916
Operation(al) Order(s)	44th Infantry Brigade Operation Order No. 90	09/09/1916	09/09/1916
Operation(al) Order(s)	44th Infantry Brigade Operation Order No. 91	09/09/1916	09/09/1916
Map	Secret Trenches To 4.9.16		
Miscellaneous	O.C. All Companies. Warning Order.	14/09/1916	14/09/1916
Miscellaneous	44th Brigade B.M. 202	14/09/1916	14/09/1916
Miscellaneous	C Form (Duplicate). Messages And Signals.		
Operation(al) Order(s)	44th Infantry Brigade Operation Order No. 94.	17/09/1916	17/09/1916
Miscellaneous	Relief Table to accompany 44th Infantry Brigade Operation Order No. 21.	17/09/1916	17/09/1916
Operation(al) Order(s)	Operation Order No 30 by Lieut Col N.A. Thomson DSO Commdg 8th Seaforth Highlanders	18/09/1916	18/09/1916
Operation(al) Order(s)	44th Infantry Brigade Operation Order No. 95	18/09/1916	18/09/1916
Miscellaneous	Relief Table to accompany 44th Infantry Brigade Operation Order No. 95	18/09/1916	18/09/1916
Operation(al) Order(s)	44th Infantry Brigade Operation Order No. 96.	18/09/1916	18/09/1916
Miscellaneous	March Table to accompany 44th Infantry Brigade Operation Order No. 96.		
Operation(al) Order(s)	44th Infantry Brigade Operation Order No. 97.	19/09/1916	19/09/1916
Miscellaneous	March Table to accompany 44th Infantry Brigade Operation Order No. 97.		
Miscellaneous	All Units 44th Infantry Brigade.	08/09/1916	08/09/1916
Map	III Corps (I)		

C O N F I D E N T I A L

WAR   DIARY.

of the

8th(Service)Battalion Seaforth Highlanders.

From 1st August 1916 to 31st August 1916.

Volume XIV.

In the Field.
31-8-1916.
..............Lieut;Colonel.
Comdg;8th(Ser)Battalion.Seaforth Highlanders.

44th Brigade.
15th Division

1/8th BATTALION

SEAFORTH HIGHALNDERS

AUGUST 1 9 1 6

Appendices 1 to 51

Report on Operations 17/18th (app XXVII
Casualties (app LI)

WAR DIARY or INTELLIGENCE SUMMARY.

Army Form C. 2118.

(Erase heading not required.)

Place	Date	Hour	Summary of Events and Information	Remarks and references to Appendices
NAOURS.	1/8/16.		Training was carried on Company arrangements. Nothing to report. Warning Order received from 11th Infantry Brigade. (Appendix I last month's diary).	Appendix I
NAOURS.	2/8/16.		Batln. in billets - training as above. Draft of 40 O.R. joined the Batln. this day.	
NAOURS.	3/8/16.		Batln. in billets - training as above.	
NAOURS.	4/8/16.		The Batln. marched from NAOURS to MIRVAUX as per attached Operation Order & march table.	Appendix II
MIRVAUX.		5.30 A.M.	Route via TALMAS - SEPTENVILLE - The Batln. was in billets by 1.30 p.m.	
MIRVAUX	5/8/16.		Batln. marched from MIRVAUX to LA HOUSSOYE as per attached Operation Order & march table. Batln. was in billets by 10 A.M. Lieut L. GYERS rejoined from hospital.	Appendix III
LA HOUSSOYE		10 A.M.	Message received from 11th I.B.	Appendix IV
LA HOUSSOYE	6/8/16.		Church Parades in the morning - Training from 5.30 p.m. to 7.30 pm under Company Arrangements.	
LA HOUSSOYE	7/8/16.		Battalion bathed at PONT NOYELLES. Training was carried on under Company Arrangements. Draft of 31 O.R. joined the Batln. this day.	

Army Form C. 2118.

WAR DIARY
or
INTELLIGENCE SUMMARY.
(Erase heading not required.)

Instructions regarding War Diaries and Intelligence Summaries are contained in F.S. Regs., Part II. and the Staff Manual respectively. Title pages will be prepared in manuscript.

Place	Date	Hour	Summary of Events and Information	Remarks and references to Appendices
LA HOUSSOYE.	8/8/16.	2.30 AM	The Battn. marched from LA HOUSSOYE to ALBERT in accordance with Operation Order & moved into attack positions in N.29.D. Central (Battalion HQrs at N.26.d.7.0.)	Appendix V. Reference ALBERT (contoured that 1/40000)
ALBERT.			The Battalion relieved 10th Battn. Northumberland Fusiliers in Divisional Reserve - relief completed by 7 a.m.	
ALBERT.	9/8/16.		Training was again carried on under company arrangements :- (Omission from 7/8/16 :- Following Officers proceeded to Divisional Reinforcement Camp at D.21.c.a.a. Lieut. H.M. POTTER, Lieut. D. GUNN, Lieut. L. BYERS, Lieut. T.G. MUIR, Lieut. M. JACKSON, Lieut. A.E. PARK, Lieut. A. McADIE, Lieut. TRR TODD, Lieut. K.A. GRANT. - Only 20 officers being allowed to accompany the Battalion into action).	ALBERT Contoured that 1/40000
ALBERT	10/8/16		Training continued under company arrangements - "A" & "B" Companies had the use of the Baths in ALBERT.	
ALBERT.	11/8/16.		The Battalion paraded for inspection by the Commanding Officer in accordance with Appendix VI. attached. A draft of 34 O.R. joined the battalion this day. A wire app. received from Maj. T.B. (attached)	Appendix VI Appendix VII

WAR DIARY
or
INTELLIGENCE SUMMARY.

Army Form C. 2118.

Place	Date	Hour	Summary of Events and Information	Remarks and references to Appendices
N. 29. d. Central. Albert (France) Sheet 1/40000	12/8/16		Battalion Headquarters is now established at N.29.d. (Central) instructions having been received that ALBERT is to be evacuated by all troops. Battalion employed on working parties as per attached appendix. Training of Lewis Gunners, Signallers, & Runners of Companies carried on as before.	Appendix VIII
N.29.d. Central	13/8/16		Battalion again employed on working parties – the same parties provided as yesterday vide Appendix VIII. Warning Order received from 44th I.B. (see attached Appendix). Nothing further to report.	Appendix IX
Scots Redoubt	14/8/16	9am	Battalion moves to Scots Redoubt as per attached operation order & march table. Battalion Headquarters being at pt. X.21.d.5.6. (Reference Map 57D. S.E. 1/20000). Working parties furnished to 44th I.B. B.M.31 attached. Coys SC.A.I.	Appendix X Appendix XI
			Appendix XII shows numbers of men left behind with 1st Line Transport.	Appendix XII
		7.45pm	Message received from 44th Inf. Bde.	Appendix XIII
		10.30pm	On going near scene of action fire of an hour – Enemy guns appeared to be replying on our front line.	Appendix XIV

Army Form C. 2118.

WAR DIARY
or
INTELLIGENCE SUMMARY.
(Erase heading not required.)

Instructions regarding War Diaries and Intelligence Summaries are contained in F.S. Regs., Part II. and the Staff Manual respectively. Title pages will be prepared in manuscript.

Place	Date	Hour	Summary of Events and Information	Remarks and references to Appendices
Scots Redoubt	15/9/16		Nothing to report - 1 heavy working party of 1 N.C.O. & 16 O.R. was supplied by "C" Company.	
Scots Redoubt Peake Wood	16/9/16		Battalion moved to PEAKE WOOD & CONTALMAISON in accordance with Operation Order No 14. Working parties supplied as per Appendix XV & XVI.	Appendix XIV Appendix XV Appendix XVI Appendix XVII
		2.15pm	Operation Order No 15 received from HQ 1st Inf Bde at 2.15pm (Appendix XVII). Battalion Operation Order No 15 issued at 5pm. Nothing further to report this day.	Appendix XVIII
Contalmaison	17/9/16	12.30pm 11.50am	Battalion moved in accordance with O.O. No 15 (see Appendix XVIII) New position occupied by 4.30am. New position: Contalmaison to North Gourlay Trench & Contalmaison Wood.	
		12 noon	1 platoon "D" Coy detailed to man up Stokes Shells & handcarts to front line.	
		12.15pm	1 platoon "A" Coy detailed to carry bombs from Contalmaison to Butterworth Trench.	
		12.50pm	"B" Coy ordered forward to BUTTERWORTH TRENCH in accordance with Inst. T.B. B.M.832.	Appendix XIX
		1pm	"D" Coy less 1 platoon replaced "B" Coy in Gourlay Trench.	
		1.30pm	1 platoon "C" Coy detailed to carry sandbags to front line.	

T2134. Wt. W708—776. 500000. 4/15. Sir J. C. & S.

Army Form C. 2118.

WAR DIARY
or
INTELLIGENCE SUMMARY.
(Erase heading not required.)

Instructions regarding War Diaries and Intelligence Summaries are contained in F. S. Regs., Part II. and the Staff Manual respectively. Title pages will be prepared in manuscript.

Place	Date	Hour	Summary of Events and Information	Remarks and references to Appendices
CONTAL MAISON	17/8/16	4 P.M.	Adjutant sent for by Brigade Major & informed that the Battalion would take over the front line from 4/2 Cameron High & 9th Black Watch during the night.	
		4 P.M.	Lieut J.A. Ross sent forward to "B" Coy to keep track when the situation in the present area.	
		6 P.M.	4th I.B. Operation Order No 14 received.	Appendix XX
		6.15 P.M.	Lieut J.A. Ross returned & reported H.Q. at about 5.30 P.M. "B" Coy were in Glasgow Alley north of Butterworth Trench & were under orders from O.C. 4/2 Cameron Highlanders to attack the Switch Elbow.	
			At this hour reports were also received that 1 Platoon "A" Coy which had been carrying bombs & 1 Platoon of "C" Coy which had been carrying Dumbings, were both in front line trenches orders of O.C. 4/2 Cameron Highrs - Both Specialist Offrs had & arrived at this hour.	Appendix XXI
		6.15 P.M.	Message received from O.C. "B" Coy that Switch Elbow had been taken & that consolidation was being carried out.	Appendix XXII Appendix XXIII
		7 P.M.	Another message from O.C. "B" Coy.	
		8 P.M.	Battn Headquarters moved to Headquarters at junction of Gorlay Trench & Yorkshire Alley.	
		9 P.M.	Another message from O.C. "B" Coy.	
		9.30 P.M.	Situation in front not at all clear & found difficult to experience in getting any information at all.	Appendix XXIV
		10 P.M.	Lt Colonel Maynd Cmdg 7th Cameron Highrs returned from front line. Situation became clearer as regards disposition of troops in front line.	

WAR DIARY
or
INTELLIGENCE SUMMARY.

(Erase heading not required.)

Army Form C. 2118.

Instructions regarding War Diaries and Intelligence Summaries are contained in F. S. Regs., Part II. and the Staff Manual respectively. Title pages will be prepared in manuscript.

Place	Date	Hour	Summary of Events and Information	Remarks and references to Appendices
Gourlay Trench	14/8/16	12 midnight	Orders issued for completion of relief of remainder of 4th Cameron by the 9th Black Watch as per first	Appendix XXV
Gourlay Trench	15/8/16	1.40 AM	"D" Coys relief complete in accordance with "D 299" (Appendix XXV)	Appendix XXVI
		2 AM	Message received from OC "B" Coy regarding portion of "B" Coy in the SWITCH ELBOW	
		2.35 AM	"C" Coys relief complete in accordance with "D 299" (Appendix XXV). Nothing further took place during the night except an intense enemy shelling of our lien etc.	
		7.35 AM	"B" Coys relief complete & the Battn in position in accordance with "D 299" (Appendix XXV). Report on attack on SWITCH ELBOW by OC "B" Coy attached.	Appendix XXVII
			During this morning the whole of the Battalion area was subjected to a very heavy bombardment by enemy guns, a number of casualties occurred including a considerable number of cases of shell shock.	
			Estimated casualties from 12 noon 14th Aug to 12 noon 15th Aug - Lieut J.H. Ross (wounded) & 50 o.r. wounds.	
		2.05 PM	At this hour "D" forty Stroke Candles were discharged along the Battalion front in accordance with instructions of Bde O.O No 96 paragraph 6. This discharge drew a very heavy fire from the enemy artillery which was continued during the whole afternoon though decreasing towards our	Appendix XXVIII

T2134. Wt. W708—776. 500000. 4/15. Sir J. C. & S.

WAR DIARY or INTELLIGENCE SUMMARY

Army Form C. 2118.

Place	Date	Hour	Summary of Events and Information	Remarks and references to Appendices
COSTREJAY TRENCH	18/8/16		Wishes & causing a number of Casualties.	Appendix X & X
			In accordance with 14th Brigade B.M. 846 & B.M. 854 arrangements were made to assist the attack of ANZACS on our immediate left.	
		Appx.	The ANZACS attacked our trenches. New our own objects to deny heavy Artillery fire by the enemy – this enemy artillery fire was specially intense on MUNSTER ALLEY & "A" Coy dugouts causing many Casualties. A great number of them were killed from shell shock. Casualties on our own lines & Vickers fire of 14th M.G. Coy were badly damaged. The intense enemy artillery fire too, kept up during the entire night.	Yes.
COSTREJAY TRENCH	19/8/16	12 am.	The enemy were seen advancing on our S.1 & 3.5 ("B" Coy front) left trenches. Our fire was at once opened on them & at 12.30 am the enemy had entirely disappeared. No further special operations were carried out during this day. Enemy artillery fire on our trenches continued practically incessantly – work on repairing & clearing damaged trenches was carried out this am greatly impeded by shell fire – the men were also by this time very much shaken by the severe bombardment. Estimated casualties from 12 noon 15/8/16 to 12 noon 19/8/16 4 Officers & 129 O.R. – Officer Casualties	

WAR DIARY or INTELLIGENCE SUMMARY.

Army Form C. 2118.

Place	Date	Hour	Summary of Events and Information	Remarks and references to Appendices
OVERLAY TRENCH	10/5/16		As follows :- Lieut D.M. CAMERON wounded, Lieut W.M. RITCHIE wounded, Lieut E.A. NAVIE wounded, Lieut R.P. SMITH Crushed & suffering from shell shock (missing) :- at 2 a.m. 1 Platoon of "D" Coy was sent up to reinforce "A" Coy on the left.	
		8 p.m.	Urgent Orders received from 44th I.B. Orders were issued to Battalion to go out along the Battalion front & assault of hostile position of the Enemy.	Appendix XXX
		8.50 p.m.	Message received from 44th I.B.	
		9 p.m.	Unusual activity on our front - Several green rockets (S-O-S Signal) were seen to go up on our right - Left & One or two were thought to go up on our front. Artillery barrage was at once established & "Stand to arms" orders	
		9.40 p.m.	Information received that the Enemy before been thought to be assembling about pt X.6.a.2.4. (opposite junction of AUSTRALIANS & "A" Company).	
		10.35 p.m.	Situation reports received from the front - Ward from HECLA Patrol (as ordered at 8p.m.) proceeds to ascertain enemy position, returns at 1.50 a.m. reports as per attached report.	Appendix XXXI
OVERLAY TRENCH	20/5/16	-	Nothing further to report during the night.	
		1.30 a.m.	The Battn. was relieved by 8th & 10th Gordon Highlanders in accordance with Operation Orders attacked. On relief which was complete at 4.30 p.m. the Battalion moved back to SCOTS REDOUBT.	Appendix XXXII

WAR DIARY
or
INTELLIGENCE SUMMARY.

Army Form C. 2118.

Place	Date	Hour	Summary of Events and Information	Remarks and references to Appendices
SCOTS REDOUBT	20/8/16		Between 17th Aug & 20th Aug. the total casualties in the battalion amounted to 5 Officers wounded, 33 OR killed, 170 OR wounded, 2 OR missing. 4 German prisoners were captured, 3 of whom gave names & were wounded. 1 belonged to 130th Regt, 1 to 176th Regt. & 2 to 179th Regt. – 3 German machine guns were also captured. Nothing further to report this day. Strength at present with the battalion – 19 Officers & 355 OR.	
SCOTS REDOUBT	21/8/16		Working parties amounting to 105 men were found by Companies to work under Brigade arrangements. 35 OR joined the battalion including several men who had been suffering from Shell Shock on 17th/18th August. Lieut N.H.GARDNER, Lieut K.H.GRANT, & Lieut T.G.MUIR joined from Reinforcement Camp.	
PEAKE WOOD	22/8/16		Battalion relieved 9th Black Watch in accordance with O.O. No.14 attached. Relief complete by 9 pm. Working parties amounting to 126 OR were found by Companies to work under Brigade arrangements. 10 OR joined the Battalion (This included 5 men returned from hospital who had been suffering from shock.	Appendix XXXIII
PEAKE WOOD	23/8/16		Working parties amounting to 140 OR supplied by batln. – Message received from D.H.Q. 1st I.B. Brigts HQrs. Nothing further to report.	Appendix XXXIV

T2184. Wt. W708—776. 500000. 4/15. Sir J. C. & S.

Army Form C. 2118.

WAR DIARY
or
INTELLIGENCE SUMMARY.
(Erase heading not required.)

Instructions regarding War Diaries and Intelligence Summaries are contained in F.S. Regs., Part II. and the Staff Manual respectively. Title pages will be prepared in manuscript.

Place	Date	Hour	Summary of Events and Information	Remarks and references to Appendices
CONTALMAISON	24/6/16		The Battn this day relieved 9th Black Watch as "B" Battn in Accordance with OO No15. Moppers Relief Complete by 8AM. Working parties Amounting to 150 O.R. Supplied by Companies.	Appendix XXXV.
			Warning Order received from H.Q. 4th I.B.	Appendix XXXVI.
		9.30pm	At about this time the Enemy fired a few Shells into CONTALMAISON. They Continued firing Gas Shells at intervals for about 1 hour. No troops casualties Occurred.	
CONTALMAISON	25/6/16		Working parties amounting to 140 O.R. supplied by the Battn. to work under Bryds Arrangements.	Appendix XXXVII.
		11 A.M.	Two messages received from H.Q. 4th I.B.	Appendix XXXVIII.
		5pm	Warning Order received from H.Q. 4th I.B. As no Orders were received to take over the portion of 45th Inf Bde front Arrangements were made to take Over the line exactly as it is held by 9th Black Watch. Draft of 104 O.R. joined the Battalion but remained at ALBERT with the 1st Line Transport.	(Vide Appendix XXXVIII).
GOURLAY TRENCH	26/6/16	3am	The Battn Commenced to relieve 9th Black Watch in front line in Accordance with Warning Order (Appendix XXXVIII)	

WAR DIARY
or
INTELLIGENCE SUMMARY.
(Erase heading not required.)

Army Form C. 2118.

Instructions regarding War Diaries and Intelligence Summaries are contained in F.S. Regs., Part II. and the Staff Manual respectively. Title pages will be prepared in manuscript.

Place	Date	Hour	Summary of Events and Information	Remarks and references to Appendices
GOURLAY TRENCH	26/8/16	1am	Relief was complete & disposition of Coy was as for Object map attached "D" on left – "C" on Right "A" in Support "B" in Reserve	Appendix XXXIX Appendix XL
		11am	44th Infy Brigade Operation No 81 was received	
		1.30pm	"A" Coy ordered to proceed to where that portion of 45th Infantry Brigade from HLI ALLEY to WELCH ALLEY "B" Coy ordered to send two platoons to LANES TRENCH formerly occupied by platoon "A" Company.	
		10am	"A" Coy relief was complete. Situation quiet normal during the morning.	
		1.50pm	Message received from 44th I.B. "B" Coy ordered to send to the platoons at present in GOURLAY TRENCH & LANES TRENCH & 6th Avenue in support of "A" Company	Appendix XLI
		3.15pm	By this hour the disposition of Coys was as per Object map attached	Appendix XLII
			The remainder of the day & night was quiet – 2nd Lieut J. KIRKWOOD wounded, 2 OR killed & 16 wounded	
			Lieut K A GRANT was killed in action, Battn Defence scheme attached	Appendix XLIII
		10pm	PATROLS went out from "C" & "D" Coys & reports as per attached report. @ patrol under 2nd Lt E M FRASER & @ under 2nd Lt L GYERS	Appendix XLIV
GOURLAY TRENCH	27/8/16	12.30pm	The early part of the morning was very quiet. Enemy Artillery were very active against GOURLAY TRENCH & our position between GOURLAY TRENCH & CONTALMAISON	

Army Form C. 2118.

WAR DIARY
or
INTELLIGENCE SUMMARY.
(Erase heading not required.)

Instructions regarding War Diaries and Intelligence Summaries are contained in F. S. Regs., Part II. and the Staff Manual respectively. Title pages will be prepared in manuscript.

Place	Date	Hour	Summary of Events and Information	Remarks and references to Appendices
GOURLAY TRENCH	2/8/16	12.30pm	Guns of all Calibre were used. Shelling appeared to come from N.E. direction. Shelling lasted for 1/2 an hour.	
		2.30pm	Enemy artillery again very active on same points as at 12.30pm. Shelling again lasted for 1/2 an hour. The afternoon was very quiet.	
		4pm	Our Guns artillery were very active on our left (i.e. to the West). It was thought action was in the direction of Thiepval. It was ascertained that operations were being carried out by the Australians on the left of the Australians (the Australian Division being on our immediate left).	
		7.30pm	The Bombardment became less intense at 7.30pm & by 8.30pm no shelling fire could be heard in that direction. Rest of the night passed quietly.	
		8PM	Message received from H.Q. 1st I.B. repeated to all companies.	Appendix XLV
GOURLAY TRENCH	3/8/16	12.30am	Patrols sent out from "A" & "C" Coy. On return reported as per attached Appendix XLVI	Appendix XLVI
		3AM	Battalion commenced being relieved by 8/10 Gordon Highrs in accordance with C.O. No.19	Appendix XLVII
		11.15AM	Relief was Complete. During the last 48 hours in the trenches work has been carried on consolidating the recently captured	

WAR DIARY or INTELLIGENCE SUMMARY.

Army Form C. 2118.

(Erase heading not required.)

Place	Date	Hour	Summary of Events and Information	Remarks and references to Appendices
			Reliefs & digging communication between firing line & strong point. A new strong post was commenced at about X.6.a.4/2.6 The dug deep enough to afford excellent cover for the garrison – this is however shot next work required in this post.	
SCOTSREDOUBT	28/8/16	8am	Batt. in SCOTS REDOUBT by 8am. Nothing particular to report during the day. Operation Order No 23 received from 86th Infantry Brigade.	Appendix XLVIII
SCOTSREDOUBT	29/8/16		Battalion had the use of Dunsapied Chaim Baths in Becourt Wood but owing to the amount of work going on only 3 companies bathed. Draft of 30 O.R. joined the Battalion today. Nothing further to report.	
SCOTSREDOUBT	30/8/16	9am	The Batt. was this day relieved by the 26th Batt. Northumberland Fusiliers in accordance with Operation Order No 20. Having been relieved by 11th Infantry Brigade Battalion proceeded to bivouac at W.29.A.6.a.	Appendix XLIX " L. "

Army Form C. 2118.

WAR DIARY
or
INTELLIGENCE SUMMARY.
(Erase heading not required.)

Instructions regarding War Diaries and Intelligence Summaries are contained in F. S. Regs., Part II. and the Staff Manual respectively. Title pages will be prepared in manuscript.

Place	Date	Hour	Summary of Events and Information	Remarks and references to Appendices
Nr Peteri N29 A 8 a	31/8/16		Working party of 300 per supplies to bring Cattle under Divisional depôt Coy. Draft of 1 Officer (Lieut T.E. Milk) & 30 OR joined for duty. Lt Col Bradley to report. Appendix LI Other Casualties for August 1916.	Appendix XLS

44th Brigade B.M.671.

Reference this office B.M.667 of 31-7-16, for 2nd August read 3rd August.

Addressed recipients of
44th Bde.O.O.No.70.
1-8-16.

[signature] Major,
Brigade Major,
44th Infantry Brigade.

COPY N°. 9

OPERATION ORDER N° 10

by
Lieut. Col. N. A. Thomson, D.S.O.
Commdg. 8th Bn. Seaforth Highlanders

August 3rd 1916

Reference Map. LENS SHEET 1/100,000.

1. The Battalion will march to new Billets to-morrow as under:—

    STARTING POINT:— "Cape de PROGRÈS, at Cross Roads 300 yards south of Church, NAOURS.

    TIME .... 4.45 a.m.

    ORDER OF MARCH ...... "C" "D" "A" and "B" Coys; Lewis Gun Detachment, 1st Line Transport (Echelon "A" and "B").

    ROUTE .... Junction 300 yards South of U of LES SOUTERRAIN.

2. Billeting party (on bicycles) of 1 N.C.O per Coy. and 1 for Headquarters will parade at 4 a.m. outside Battn. Headquarters under 2/Lieut. J. H. Ross — special instructions have been issued to him.

3. Officers Valises will be taken to Quartermasters Stores by 4 a.m. to-morrow — mess Boxes will be collected at 4.15 a.m.

4. 2/Lieut. A. McAdie will march behind Echelon "B", 1st Line Transport and in all details, other than drivers and brakesmen, will be marched in a formed body by him, behind the Transport.

    The Transport Officer will send all men who join the Transport on the march to report to this Officer.

5. Refilling point will be notified later.

6. The attention of all concerned is called to this Office N° A/8 d/30.7.16 re. March Discipline.

George O. Duncan.
Capt.,
Adjutant, 8th Seaforth Highlanders.

Distribution.

Copy N° 1. O.C. "A" Coy.
       2. O.C. "B" Coy.
       3. O.C. "C" Coy.
       4. O.C. "D" Coy.
       5. Lewis Gun Officer.
       6. Transport Officer.
       7. 2/Lieut. J. H. Ross.
       8. Headquarters Mess.

March Table to accompany 44th Infantry Brigade Operation Order No.71. dated 3-8-1916.

UNITS. In order of march.	STARTING POINT. Place.	Time. A.M.	ROUTE.	DESTINATION.
44th Bde.H.Q. and Signal Secn:	Road	4-30	TALMAS -	MIRVAUX.
9th Black Watch.	Junction	4-31		"
8/10th Gordon Hrs.	300 yards	4-42	SEPTENVILLE.	"
8th Seaforth Hrs.	South of	5-3		"
7th Cameron Hrs.	U of LES	5-14		"
44th T.M.Battery.	SOUTERRAINS.	5-25		"
44th M.G.Coy.		5-26		"
91st Fld.Coy.R.E.		5-35		PIERREGOT.
9th Gordon Hrs. (Pioneers)		5-43		"
46th Fld.Amb. (Less 1 Section).		6-4		EBART FARM (Not marked). 1/3rd mile N.W. of A of AGNICOURT.

OPERATION ORDER No B

Lieut. Col. N. A. by Thomson, D.S.O.
Commdg. 8th Bn. Seaforth Highlanders

Copy No 9

Aug. 4th 1916

Reference Map. LENS SHEET 1/10,000
AMIENS SHEET 1/100,000

III

1. The Battalion will march South East to new billets to-morrow as under:-
   - STARTING POINT — Church, MIRVAUX
   - TIME — 7.10 a.m.
   - ORDER OF MARCH — "D", "A", "B" and "C" Coys, Lewis Gun Detachment, 1st Line Transport (Echelon "A" and "B".)

2. Billeting party (on bicycles) of 1 N.C.O per Coy. and 1 for Headquarters will parade outside Battn. H.Q. at 6·50 am under 2/Lieut. J. A. Ross - special instructions will be issued to him.

3. Officer's valises will be taken to Quartermaster's stores by 6·20 a.m. to-morrow. mess boxes will be collected at 6·40 a.m.

4. 2/Lieut. E. M. Fraser will march behind Echelon "B" 1st Line Transport, and all details, other than Drivers and Brakesmen will be marched in a formed body by him behind the Transport. The Transport Officer will send all men who join the Transport on the march, to report to this officer.

5. Refilling point will be notified later.

George W. Duncan
Capt.,
Adjutant, 8th Bn. Seaforth Highrs.

Distribution
- Copy. No 1 — O.C. "A" Coy.
- " 2 — O.C. "B" Coy.
- " 3 — O.C. "C" Coy.
- " 4 — O.C. "D" Coy.
- " 5 — Lewis Gun Officer.
- " 6 — Transport Officer.
- " 7 — 2/Lt. J. A. Ross
- " 8 — Headquarters Mess.
- " 9 — War Diary
- " 10 — File

March Table to accompany 44th Infantry Brigade Operation Order No.73, dated 1-8-16.

Units. In order of march.	STARTING POINT. Place.	Time.	ROUTE.	DESTINATION.
44th Bde.H.Q. and Signal Scn:	~~Western~~ Eastern end of MIRVAUX.	A.M. 7-0	First R of BEAUCOURT-SUR-L'HALLUE – road junction ¼ mile S.W of B of BAVILINCOURT – First R of FRECHINCOURT. (Units for LA HOUSSOYE to clear BEHENCOURT by 10 A.M. after which hour roads to be kept clear for Div.H.Q. and 19th Div. Artillery.	Chateau, BEHENCOURT.
9th Black Watch.		7-1		LA HOUSSOYE.
8th Seaforth Hrs.		7-12		
7th Cameron Hrs.		7-23		
8/10th Gordon Hrs.		7-34		
44th M.G.Coy.		7-45		BEHENCOURT.
44th T.M.Battery.		8-3		
9th Gordons (Pioneers).		8-9		
91st Fld.Coy.R.E.		8-20		

SECRET.   44th Bde.B.M.28.

44th Brigade Group.

Following message received from 15th Division is forwarded for your information.-

"WARNING ORDER AAA 46th relieve 70 Inf.Bde. in right on 7th instant AAA 44th relieve 68th Inf. Bde. in reserve morning of 8th instant AAA 45th relieve 69th in left on 8th inst AAA Field Companies will relieve with brigades AAA Pioneers relieve on 8th AAA Orders follow.

                                W.G. Wright Captain,
                                  for Brigade Major,
                                  44th Infantry Brigade.
5-8-16.

-Secret-   **OPERATION – ORDER No. 12**
                                                                    Copy. 10

Lieut. Col. N. A. 8/th 0112-0012, D.S.O.
Commanding 8th (S) Battalion Seaforth Highlanders

— Aug. 7th 1916 —

Reference Map.
AMIENS 1/100,000 Sht. 17. TRENCH MAP Sht 57d.S.E

I. The Battalion will march to ALBERT to-morrow to relieve the 10th Battn. NORTHUMBERLAND FUSILIERS as under:—

   STARTING POINT ..... North Eastern Exit of LA HOUSSOYE
   TIME .... 2.34 a.m.
   ORDER OF MARCH ..... "A", "B", "C" and "D" Coys, Lewis Gun Detachment, 1st Line Transport, Echelon "A" and "B".
   ROUTE .... Main AMIENS-ALBERT Road.

II. The Battalion will Bivouac in W.29.D. Central.

III. Officers' Valises will be taken to Quartermaster's Stores by 1.30 a.m. to-morrow; mess boxes will be collected at 1.30 a.m.

IV. 2/Lieut. R. A. Berry-Hart will march behind Echelon "B", 1st Line Transport: all details other than drivers and Brakesmen will be marched by him in a formed body.

The Transport Officer will send all men who join the Transport on the march to report to this Officer.

                        George W. Duncan. Capt.
                        Adjutant, 8th Battn Seaforth Highrs.

Distribution- Copy. No 1. O.C "A" Coy.
             2. O.C "B" Coy.
             3. O.C "C" Coy.
             4. O.C "D" Coy.
             5. Transport Officer
             6. Quartermaster
             7. Lewis Gun Officer
             8. Signalling Officer
             9. Medical Officer
            10. War Diary
            11. File.

March Table to accompany 11th Infantry Brigade Operation Order No.73, dated 6th August,1916.

UNIT.	STARTING POINT.		ROUTE.	DESTINATION.	Unit of 68th Inf.Bde. to be relieved.	REMARKS.
	PLACE	TIME A.M.				
11th Inf.Bde. H.Q. and Signal Secn:	North	2-0	Main	ALBERT.		Units at ECHELCOURT to march to Starting Point via road passing through E of FRECHECOURT. (2). Baggage wagons of units to move via POST ROYHEATS and to be timed to join their units at the Starting Point.
8/10th Gordon Hrs.	Eastern	2-1	AMIENS	Bivouac X.26 Central. O.B.1.	11th North:Fusrs.	
9th Black Watch.	Exit	2-12		Bivouac E.5.b.O.4.	12th D.L.I.	
7th Cameron Hrs.	of LA	2-23	ALBERT	Bivouac W.30 C & D. Near Shamrock Tree.	13th D.L.I.	
8th Seaforth Hrs.	HOUSSOYE.	2-31	Road.	Bivouac W.29 D.Central.	10th North: Fusrs.	
11th M.G.Coy. 11th T.M.Battery. 9th Gordon Hrs. (Pioneers).		2-15 3-3		Bivouac E.3.C. Bivouac BECOURT WOOD.	{68th M.G.Coy. {68th T.M.Batty. 9th S.Staffords. (Pioneers).	
91st Field Coy.R.E.		3-11		- do -		

8th Seaforth Hrs.   D/244.   1/10/16.

O.C. all Coys.
Lewis Gun Officer.
Signalling Officer
Transport Officer

VI

The Battalion will parade to-morrow at 10 a.m. for Inspection by the Commanding Officer.

DRESS will be that laid down in this Office D. 243 of to-day's date.

The Quartermaster will start issuing equipment at 8.30 a.m. to-morrow.

Place of Parade as communicated to Company Commanders to-day.

George W. Duncan Capt.
Adjutant, 8th Seaforth Highrs.

8·1/2 (S) Bn Seaforth Hrs. — D/243 — 10/8/16.

O.C. all Coys.
Lewis Gun Officer
Transport Officer
Quartermaster.
Signalling Officer

When the Battalion moves, the following dress will be adopted:—

(1) The dress will be marching Order less packs and greatcoats, with the following additions:—

(a) <u>Bombers.</u> — Every Bomber will carry 50 rounds S.A.A. and 12 Bombs; 6 bombs being carried in the pouches and 6 in two Satchels which will be worn over the haversack and under the right and left arm-pit respectively. The 50 rounds S.A.A. will be carried over the haversack, and underneath the right arm-pit, the S.A.A. lying just underneath the left pouch.

Every Bomber will also carry 2 sandbags — a sandbag being carried underneath each brace, just above the pouch.

(b) <u>All ranks excluding Bombers</u>:—

Every man will carry 220 rounds S.A.A.: 120 of which will be carried as formerly in the pouches, and 100 rounds will be carried in bandoliers of 50, the bandoliers being worn over the haversack and under the right and left arm-pit respectively.

Every man will carry 2 Bombs; these bombs will be placed in the foot of a sandbag; the sandbag will then be rolled up, and another sandbag rolled round it. The bundle will then be placed on the right pouch, and tied on to the right brace.

(c) 50% of each company will carry ½ picks and ½ shovels. These tools will be carried underneath the haversack, with the head of the tool just behind the head of the man.

(d) <u>Gas Helmets</u> will be worn as follows:—
The <u>P.H. helmet</u> will be worn as for "Gas Alert".
The <u>P.H.G. helmet</u> will be worn in the satchel as a sporran.
The <u>Gas Goggles</u> will be worn round the neck.
The <u>spare satchel</u> will be carried in the Haversack.

(e) <u>All Officers</u> will wear the Kilt.

(f) <u>All ranks</u> will wear Shrapnel Helmets.

George W. Duncan, Capt,
Adjutant, 8th Seaforth Highlanders

Aug. 10th 1916.

O.C. All Companies
    Lewis Gun Officer
        Transport Officer
           Quartermaster
              Signalling Officer

D243/1

1. Reference this office D243 d/10-8-16, re dress. Please amend as follows :-

    Para (1) (a) - The 50 rounds S.A.A. will be carried over the haversack & underneath the left armpit, the S.A.A. lying just underneath the right pouch.

    Para (1) (b) line 6 - The 2 bombs will be rolled in one sandbag and placed in the spare gas helmet satchel. The satchel will be worn over the haversack and underneath the left armpit - the satchel lying underneath the bandolier of S.A.A. The second sandbag will be tucked into the front of the belt behind the centre buckle.

2. Please add the following :-

    (a) 2 picks & 2 shovels will be carried with each Lewis Gun team.

    (b) 4 picks & 4 shovels will be carried by the Signal Section.

    (c) Any men who may be left behind when the Battalion moves, must be equipped the same as any private soldier as laid down in Para 1 (a) of the above letter, ready to join their Companies at a moments notice.

12-8-16

George H. Duncan. Captain
Adjt. 8th Battn Seaforth Highlanders

VII

SECRET.   44th Brigade B.M.743.

All Units 44th Inf.Bde.

1. Offensive Operations are to be carried out by 45th and 46th Infantry Brigades on night of 12/13th. (See special Operation Map attached).

    44th Infantry Brigade remains in Divisional Reserve but will move into positions of readiness on 12th instant as under :-

8/10th Gordon Hrs.	to PEAK Wood.
9th Black Watch.	to SCOTS REDOUBT.
7th Cameron Hrs.	to O.B. in X. 26. a.
8th Seaforth Hrs.	Stand fast.

    44th M.G.Coy. and 44th T.M.Battery to Camp now occupied by 9th Black Watch. (Pt.E.5.b.7.7.).

2. Units will be ready to move at ~~three~~ ½ an hours notice from 12 NOON, 12th August.

    The order to move and the hour by which the movement is to be completed, will be notified later.

3. Brigade Headquarters does not move.

                                    E a Beck
                                    Major,
                                    Brigade Major,
                                    44th Infantry Brigade.

11-8-16.

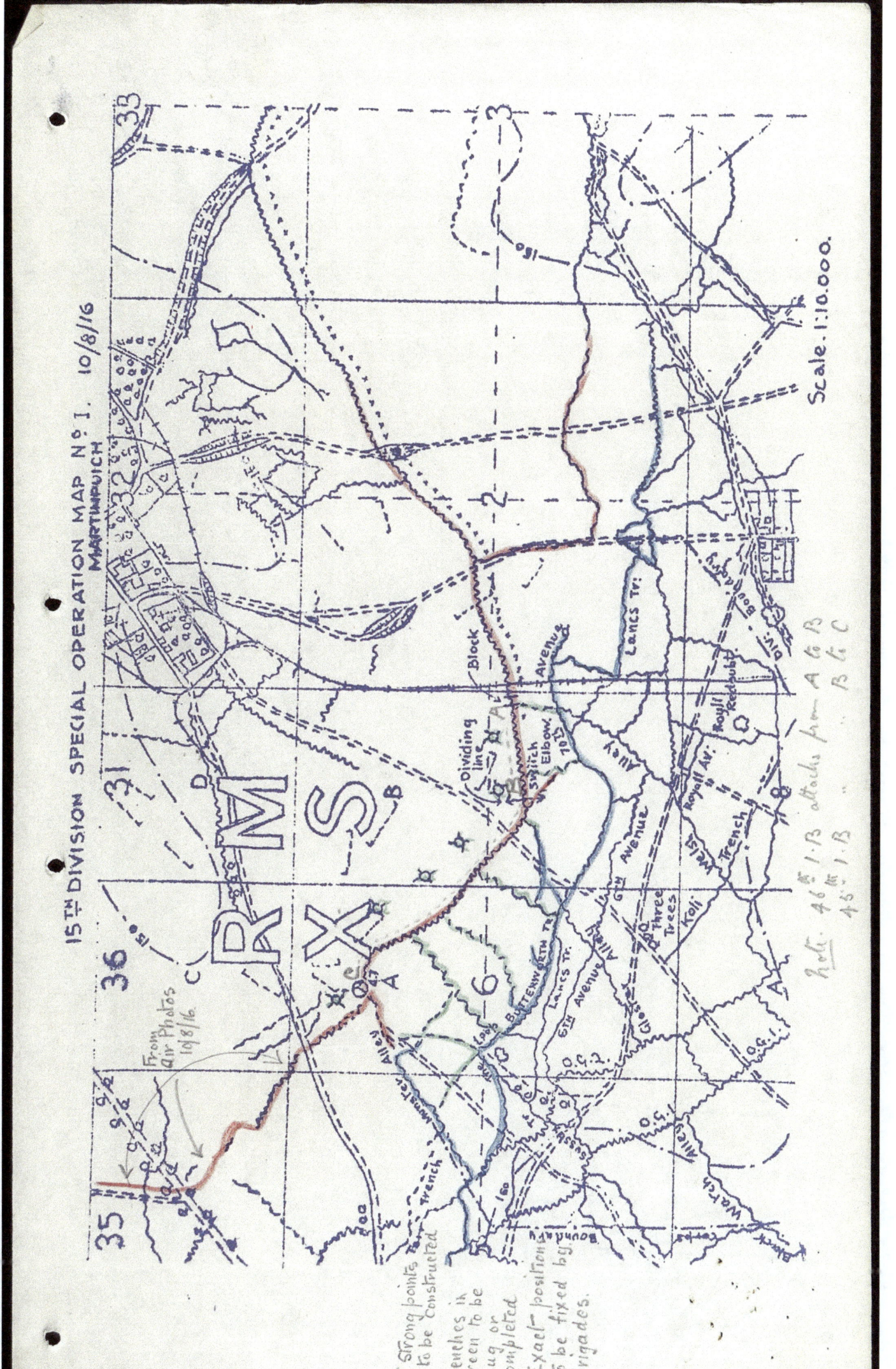

W. DIARY

VIII

O.C. ALL COYS.

1. The following working parties will be supplied by Companies as under:—

(a) 2 Officers + 100 men ...... "A" Coy.
    2 Officers + 100 men ...... "B" Coy.
    This party to report to Signal Officer 7th Heavy Artillery Group at F.1.C.4 at 9 A.M.   Party will be under Capt: G. MURRI

(b) 2 Officers + 100 men ...... "C" Coy.
    This party to report to Signal Officer 34th H.A.G at X.25.B.4.5 (Road leading from BECOURT to LA BOISSELLE) at 9 A.M.

(c) 1 Officer + 50 men ...... "D" Coy.
    This party will report to a representative of 74th Field Coy R.E. at "F" Dump E.9.d. Central at 6 A.M.

(d) 1 Officer + 50 men ...... "D" Coy.
    This party will report to a representative of 74th Field Coy, R.E at F.3.d.1.3 at 6 A.M.

2. PARTIES (a) + (b) will be employed burying Cables for III Corps.
   PARTIES (c) + (d) will be employed constructing Concertina wire and will work from 6 A.M till 11 A.M.

George W. Duncan Captain
Adjutant, 8th Battalion Seaforth Highlanders

HEADQUARTERS.
Date 11/8/16
No. A13
8th. (S) Battn. Seaforth Highrs.

"A" Form.
MESSAGES AND SIGNALS.   Army Form C. 2121.

Prefix	Code	Words	Charge	This message is on a/c of:	Recd. at
SECRET			Sent		Date
	S.D.R.	At	m.	Service.	From
		To			
		By		(Signature of "Franking Officer.")	By

TO { 8" Seaforth Hrs.

Sender's Number	Day of Month	In reply to Number	
Bm 763	13	-	AAA

Warning order aaa. Your Battalion will move tomorrow morning to SCOTS REDOUBT leaving your present position at 9 a.m. aaa operation orders will be issued later

From 44. I.B.
Place
Time 5.50 pm

Lassack Major

Bde Major
44 I.B.

SECRET

OPERATION ORDER. No 13
by
Lieut. Col. N. A. Thomson, D.S.O.
— Commdg 8th (S) Battn. Seaforth Highlanders —

COPY No. 9

Reference.
57 D.S.E. 1/20,000.

Aug 13th 1916

1. The Battalion will move to SCOTS REDOUBT, to-morrow as under:—
   - STARTING POINT:— Battn. Guard Tent.
   - TIME .... 9 a.m.
   - Order of March. Headquarters Signallers, "B" "C" "D" and "A" Coys, Headquarters Lewis Gun Detachment.
   - Route .... Main BECOURT- FRICOURT ROAD.

   All movements to be by platoons at 250 yds intervals.

2. Advanced parties of 1 N.C.O per Coy. and 1 for Headquarters, will parade with Bicycles outside Battn. H.Q. at 6.45 a.m under 2/Lieut. J. H. Ross. These parties will meet their respective Coys. on the main Road between BECOURT and FRICOURT and guide them to their position.

3. Travelling kitchens and watercarts will accompany the Battalion. — Mess-Boxes will be collected at 9 a.m — 1 limber will be outside Battn. H.Q. at 9.15 a.m. The Transport Officer will arrange that these vehicles proceed with a suitable interval between each.

4. All packs and great-coats and Officers Valises will be stacked in Camp under Coy. arrangements. The Transport Officer will arrange to Transport them to Quartermasters Stores.

5. 1st Line Transport and Quartermasters Stores will remain in their present position.

Distribution.
Copy No. 1. OC "A" Coy.
2. OC "B" Coy.
3. OC "C" Coy.
4. OC "D" Coy.
5. Lewis Gun Officer
6. 2/Lieut. J. H. Ross
7. Transport Officer
8. Quartermaster
9. War Diary
10. File.

George W. Duncan
Capt.
Adjutant, 8th Bn. Seaforth Highrs

S E C R E T.   Copy No. 2

44th Infantry Brigade Operation Order No. 74.

13-8-16.

Reference :-
   57.D.S.E. 1/20,000.
   Revised Trench Tracing
   Sheet No.7. 1/10,000.
   ALBERT (Combined Sheet) 1/40,000.

1. The 44th Infantry Brigade will relieve the 45th Infantry Brigade in the Left Section of Left Sector III Corps on the 14th August, in accordance with attached relief table.

2. 220 rounds S.A.A., 2 bombs, 2 sandbags per man, and 50% of picks and shovels to be carried.

3. All movements to be by platoons at suitable intervals.

4. The relief of "A" Battalion will be carried out at the discretion of G.O.C.45th Inf.Bde.
   In case of interruption, the relief of the remaining battalions will proceed as per table.

5. Battalion 1st Line Transport will remain in present position.

6. Completion of reliefs to be reported by wire to Brigade H.Qrs, which will move to CONTALMAISON at 11 A.M.

                                         E.A.Beck. Major,
                                                  Brigade Major,
Issued at   44th Infantry Brigade.
8 P.M.
Through Signals.

                Copies to :-
                    No. 1. 9th Black Watch.
                        2. 8th Seaforth Hrs.
                        3. 8/10th Gordon Hrs.
                        4. 7th Cameron Hrs.
                        5. 44th M.G.Coy.
                        6. 44th T.M.Battery.
                        7. 45th Inf.Bde.
                        8. 46th Inf.Bde.
                        9. 12th Aust.Inf.Bde.
                       10. 15th Division.
                       11. 91st Fld.Coy.R.E.
                       12. Bde.Transport Officer.
                       13. Bde.Supply Officer.
                       14. No.2 Coy.Train.
                       15. Bde.Signal Officer.
                       16. Staff Capt.
                       17. War Diary.
                       18. File.
                       19. 15th D.A.
                       20. 23rd D.A.
                       21. III Corps D.A.

Relief Table to accompany 44th Infantry Brigade Operation Order No. 71.

Unit 44th Inf.Bde. Now at -	Unit 45th Inf.Bde. Now at -	Guides (1 per Coy.) PLACE.	TIME. A.M.	Route for Units relieving.	REMARKS.
8/10th Gordon Hrs. ("A" Battn.) SCOTS REDOUBT.	6th Cameron Hrs. ("A" Battn.) Front Line. Support.	H.Q. 8/10th Gordons.	4-0	Most convenient.	Guides will be from 6th Camerons and 6/7th R.Scots Fusrs:
9th Black Watch. ("B" Battn.)	6/7th R.S.Fusrs: ("B" Battn.)	On FRICOURT - CONTALMAISON Road at Round Wood.	6-0	- do -	9th Black Watch to be disposed 2 Co's (less 1 platoon) in GOURLAY Trench, 1 platoon CONTALMAISON Villa. H.Q. and 2 Co's CONTALMAISON
7th Cameron Hrs. ("C" Battn.)	11th A.& S.Hrs. ("C" Battn.)	As above.	8-0	- do -	7th Cameron Hrs. to be disposed - 2 Co's (less 2 platoons) CONTALMAISON. 1 platoon.) In each of 1 Lewis) strong points, gun.) Cutting, and N.W. corner CONTALMAISON H.Q. & 2 Co's PEAKE WOOD.
8th Seaforth Hrs. ("D" Battn.)	2 Co's 9th Black 8/10th Gordons (less 2 Co's) SCOTS REDOUBT.	Not required.	---	To leave present bivouac at 9 A.M.	
44th T.M.Batty.	45th T.M.Battery.	On early morning of 14th under arrangements to be made between O.C.Batteries concerned.			1 man per mortar to be attached to 45th T.M.Battery for to-night.
44th M.G.Coy.	45th M.G.Coy.	On evening of 13th under arrangements to be made between O.C.Co's concerned.			No.1 of each gun 45th M.G. Coy. to remain until dawn 14th instant.

"A" Form.
MESSAGES AND SIGNALS.
Army Form C. 2121

Prefix	Code	Words	Charge	This message is on a/c of:	Recd. at ___ m.
		52		Service.	Date
Office of Origin and Service Instructions.		Sent			From
A.R.		At ___ m.			By
		To		(Signature of "Franking Officer")	
		By			

TO — FOAL PONY XI

* Sender's Number.	Day of Month	In reply to Number	AAA
B.M.31.	13		

Please detail two reliefs each
of 1 officer and 24 O.R. to
proceed with picks and shovels
to 45th Bde H.Q. CONTALMAISON
to-morrow 12th AAA First relief
to report at 8 A.M. second relief
at 1 P.M. AAA Both parties
to report to 44th Bde.
Signal Officer.

From HORSE
Place
Time 7.20 p.m.   E.a.B.

The above may be forwarded as now corrected. (Z)

Censor. Signature of Addressor or person authorised to telegraph in his name.
* This line should be erased if not required.

"A" Form.
MESSAGES AND SIGNALS.
Army Form C. 2121.

Prefix	Code	m.	Words	Charge	This message is on a/c of:	Recd. at _____ m.
Office of Origin and Service Instructions.			Sent		Service.	Date
SDR			At _____ m.			From
			To			By
			By		(Signature of "Franking Officer.")	

TO 8th Seaforths.

Sender's Number.	Day of Month	In reply to Number	
SC. A/1.	14th		AAA

Please detail a carrying party of 1 NCO. and 7 men to draw the following from "C" Dump CONTALMAISON & carry to Bde Bomb Store CONTALMAISON VILLA & hand over to NCO in charge there as soon as possible.

Very Lights (white) 1½" — 2 Boxes.
  "   "   "   1" — 4   "
  "   "   Green.   1   "

W.G. Wright Capt
  Staff Capt

From 44. IB.
Place
Time 4 pm.

Officers Commanding,
All Companies.
Lewis Gun Officer
Transport Officer
Quartermaster

XII

When the battalion moves the following personnel will remain with 1st Line Transport.

Regtl. Quartermaster Sergeant.
4 Company Quartermaster Sergeants.
Master Tailor.
Master Shoemaker and 2 Shoemakers.
Pipers and Drummers (except 2 pipers & 2 drummers)
Orderly Room Sergeant
1 Clerk.
1 Policeman
2 Quartermaster's Storemen.
1 Butcher.
Transport Personnel
48 Reserve Lewis Gunners.
Servants (Transport Officer & Quartermaster)

All other N.C.O's and men will accompany the battalion & on no account is the above list to be added to.

George W. Duncan. Captain
Adjt. 8th Battn. Seaforth Highlanders

12-8-16

"C" Form (Original).
MESSAGES AND SIGNALS.   Army Form C. 2123

Prefix SM Code GH^{pm} Words 29	Received From BDE By Buller	Sent, or sent out At .... m. To .... By	Office Stamp. PONY 14/8/16
Charges to collect £ s. d.			
Service Instructions. AR	XIII		

Handed in at HORSE SIGNALS Office 7.40 p.m. Received 7.46 p.m.

TO PONY

Sender's Number BM 783	Day of Month 14TH	In reply to Number	AAA
Corps	wire	AAA	Enemy suspected
of	assembling	to	attack ANZAC
right	AAA	8/10TH	GORDONS and
44TH	M.G.	COY	to be prepared
to	render	all	possible
assistance			

FROM PLACE & TIME HORSE 7.30 PM

SECRET

COPY N°7

OPERATION ORDER N°14
by
Lieut. Col. N. A. Thomson, D.S.O.
Commdg. 8th Bn. Seaforth Highlanders

XIV

15th August 1916.

Ref. Sheet 57d. S.E. 1/20,000

1. The Battalion will relieve 7th Cameron Highrs. in "C" area to-morrow as follows:—
   Coys. will relieve the corresponding Coys of 7th Cameron Highrs.
   "A" Coy. in PEAKE WOOD TRENCH
   "B" Coy. in   "   "
   "C" Coy. in CONTALMAISON with 1 platoon and 1 Lewis Gun in strong point at N.W. corner of CONTALMAISON.
   "D" Coy. in CONTALMAISON with 1 platoon and 1 Lewis Gun in the CUTTING
   Headquarters in PEAKE WOOD (Pt. X. 22.a. 8. 7½)

2. Coys. will move from present position as follows:—
   ORDER of MARCH — "D", "C", "B" and "A" Coys, Headquarters Lewis Gun Detatchment.

   TIME — 4.30 a.m.
   All movements to be by platoons at 5 mins. interval

3. Cookers will accompany Companies — O.C. Coys. are responsible for finding cover or shelter for their own Cookers

4. Mess boxes will be moved by fatigue parties under Coy. arrangements.

5. Men may take great coats — O.C. Coys. will arrange on arrival at new positions, to select a shelter where the greatcoats may be dumped in the event of the Battn. being ordered forward unexpectedly

6. O.C. "B" Coy. will arrange to relieve guard of 1 N.C.O and 9 men at Bde. H.Q. at present supplied by "B" Coy. 7th Cameron H'rs.

Copies No 1. O.C. "A" Coy.   5 Lewis Gun officer
       2. O.C. "B" "   6 Transport officer
       3. O.C. "C" "   7 War Diary
       4. O.C. "D" "   8 File

George W. Duncan
Adjutant 8th Seaforth H'rs. Capt.

U R G E N T.

XV

44th Brigade.
B.M. 800.

O. C., 9th Black Watch,
    8th Seaforth Highrs.,
    8/10th Gordon Highrs.,
    7th Cameron Highrs.,

    15th Divnl. Signl. Coy. - for information.

"D" Battalion, commencing with the 8th Seaforths to-morrow 16th instant, will find the following working party daily :-

2 Officers and 130 men to report to an Officer of 15th Divisional Signal Company at 10 A.M. at Point S.1,d, 6.2. (Junction of WELCH ALLEY and SIXTH AVENUE).

Haversack rations and tools - half shovels, half picks - will be carried.

15th August 1916.

                              Major,
                          Brigade Major,
                        44th Infantry Brigade.

"C" Form (Original).
MESSAGES AND SIGNALS.

Army Form C. 2123

Prefix SM	Code EAPM	Words 58	Received From BDE By Clifford	Sent, or sent out At .... m. To .... By	Office Stamp PONY 15/8/16 S^T N CLIFF
Charges to collect £ s. d.					
Service Instructions. AK					

Handed in at HORSE SIGS Office 5... m. Received 5.30 m.

TO D M XVI

*Sender's Number	Day of Month	In reply to Number	
BM796	15TH		AAA

Please detail two working parties tomorrow 16TH each of 1 officer and 35 men to rendezvous at the CUTTING CONTAEMAISON at 5.30 AM and 6 AM respectively to clean and deepen GLOSTER ALLEY between OG2 and BUTTERWORTH TRENCH under 73RD RE AAA parties will bring half picks and half shovels AAA Acknowledge

FROM AK
PLACE & TIME 4.55 PM

XVII

S E C R E T.   COPY No. 2

44th Infantry Brigade Operation Order No.75.
───────────────────────────────
                                              16-8-16.
Reference.
15th Divn.Map No.3
   d/14-8-16. 1/5000.

1. 44th Infantry Brigade will attack German trench line
    between the points S.1.d.4.8. and X.6.a.7.3. on 17th instant
    at an hour to be notified later.

2. 7th Cameron Hrs. will find the assaulting party.

    III Corps H.A., 34th Div.Arty., 46th T.M.Battery and 46th
    M.G.Coy. will co-operate as indicated below.-

3.(a) Action by 7th Cameron Hrs.
    (i) Dig a trench parallel to German line at a distance of
    about 100 yards from it, running from GLOSTER Alley to
    Boyau joining BUTTERWORTH Trench and New Switch. Work to
    be completed by 6 A.M. 17th.

    (ii) Assaulting party to be in position in this trench
    half-hour before "ZERO" hour, organised as covering party
    with Lewis guns, clearing party and digging party.

    (iii) At "ZERO" hour to rush German trench.

    (iv) (a) The covering party will push on as far as our
    barrage permits.
    (b) The clearing party will clear trenches and
    establish double blocks at about S.1.d.4.8. and
    X.6.a.9.3.(if necessary).
    (c) The digging party will commence the construction of
    strong points at about S.1.b.0.3. S.1.b.1.1. X.6.a.9.3.
    A special party will be detailed to join GLOSTER Sap
    to the German line.
    O.C.73rd Fld.Coy.R.E. will detail parties to supervise
    and assist in the construction of strong points and
    blocks.
    Wire for wiring the strong points will be collected
    under Brigade arrangements at junctions of Boyaux and
    new trench mentioned in para 3.(a) (i).
    (v) As soon as the trench has been cleared of Germans,
    all men not required for covering, digging, or holding
    the trench, will be withdrawn into our original lines.
    (vi) Dress. Fighting order. Sufficient food and water
    for 24 hours will be carried.

(b) Action by 9th Black Watch.
    (i) Clear GLOSTER Alley and BUTTERWORTH Trench, up to Boyau
    leading to New Switch, of troops by 7 A.M.
    (ii) Detail a party to connect point X.6.a.8.2. to German
    line about X.6.a.9.3.
    This party will be ready to commence work as soon as the
    German trench has been carried.

                        (1.)
                                              P.T.O.

(c). Action by 44th T.M.Battery.

(i) At "ZERO" hour establish a barrage on German trench about S.1.d.5.8. This barrage will be maintained until O.C.7th Cameron Hrs. decides that it is no longer necessary.
(ii) At "ZERO" hour establish an intense bombardment of German trench from about X.6.a.9.1½. to a. 9.3. This bombardment will cease when the Artillery barrage lifts.

46th T.M.Battery will co-operate at zero hour by bombarding German line from point S.1.d.5.8. Eastwards to railway. Bombardment to continue to + 15 minutes.

(d) Action by 44th M.G.Coy.

(i) To cover the flank of the attack from Point X.6.a.0.5. to the east, and to be ready to take advantage of all targets which may present themselves.
(ii) To keep down hostile fire which may come from snipers in shell holes east of GLOSTER Alley, and S. of German trench.

46th M.G.Coy. will co-operate to the east.

4. In the event of the Reserve Coy. of 7th Cameron Hrs. being drawn into the fight, 9th Black Watch will re-occupy the trenches vacated by them.

5. 8th Seaforth Hrs. will move 2 Companies to GOURLAY Trench from which two platoons will be detailed to be ready to carry bombs and S.A.A. from CONTALMAISON VILLA to BUTTERWORTH Trench.
H.Qrs. and 2 Companies to CONTALMAISON. Move to be complete by 7 A.M. 17th instant.

6. Prisoners will be sent to Collecting Station at X.28.b.2.6.

7. Outline of Artillery action.   34th Divisional Artillery.

(i) At zero hour open an intense barrage 20 yards in front German trench from S.2.a.9.4. to X.6.a.9.3.
(ii) At plus 1 minute to lift on front of attack to 120 yards and forming a box round area being consolidated.

(iii) Maintain barrage on rest of German line.

(iv) Deal with dangerous points in area.

Corps Artillery.
Shell road cutting in S.2.a., MARTINPUICH, strong points about X.6.a.2.9. and R.35.b.4.4. with H.A. and gas shells.

Deal with dangerous points in area.

LaBeck Major,
Brigade Major,
44th Infantry Brigade.

Issued Through
Signals. 130 P.M.

Copy No. 1. 9th Black Watch.   10. 15th Div.Arty.
2. 8th Seaforth Hrs.   11. 34th Div.Arty.
3. 8/10th Gordon Hrs.   12. 73rd Fld.Coy.R.E.
4. 7th Cameron Hrs.   13. 46th Fld.Amb.
5. 44th M.G.Coy.   14. Bde.Signal Section.
6. 44th T.M.Battery.   15. 9th Gordons (Pioneers).
7. 15th Div.   16. Staff Captain.
8. 46th Inf.Bde.   17. War Diary.
9. 4th Aust. Inf.Bde.   18. File.

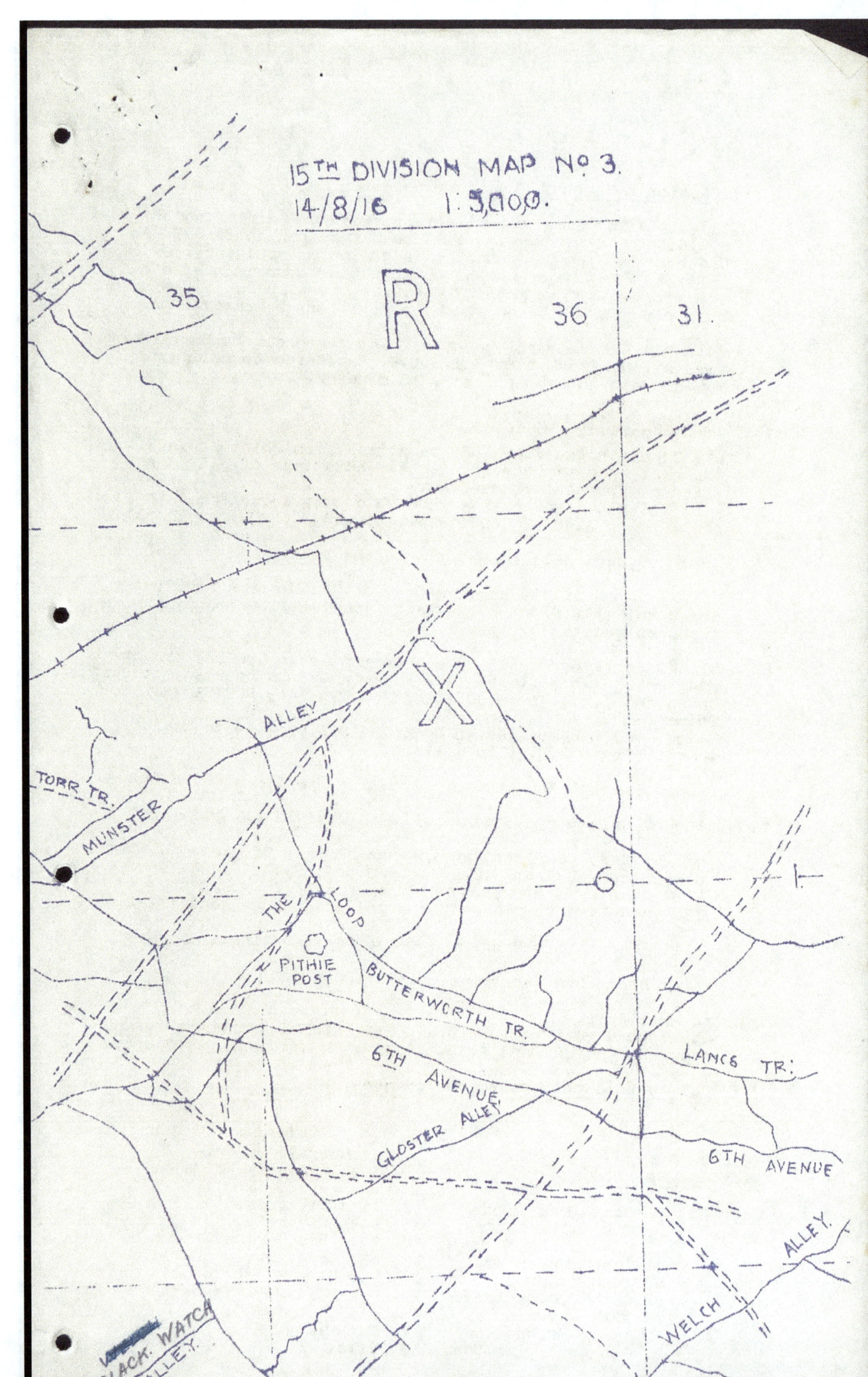

SECRET

OPERATION ORDER No 15
by
Lieut. Col. N.M. Thomson D.S.O.
Commdg. 8th (S) Bn. Seaforth Highlanders

Ref. 15th Div. Map. of 14.8.16
1/5000 and SHEET 57 d S.E.

No. 6

I. The 44th Infantry Brigade will attack the German Trenches line between S.1.d.4.8 and X.6.a.7.3. on 17th inst. at an hour to be notified later.

The assault is to be carried out by the 7th Cameron Hrs. who will pass through 9th Black Watch who are at present holding the front line.

2. "A" and "B" Coys. 8th Seaforth Hrs. will relieve C & D Coys 7th Cameron Hrs. to-morrow in the following order:-

<u>A Coy.</u> will relieve C Coy. 7th Cameron Hrs. in GOURLAY TRENCH with 1 platoon and 1 Lewis Gun in CONTALMAISON VILLA.

<u>B Coy.</u> will relieve D Coy. 7th Cameron Hrs. in GOURLAY TRENCH.

All movements will be by platoons at 5 mins interval:-

Leading Platoon of "A" Coy. will move off at 5.45 a.m.

Relief of both Coys. to be complete by 7 a.m.

- 2 -

off at 5.45 a.m.
Relief of both Coys. to be complete by 7
C & D Coys 8th Seaforth Htrs. will remain in
present positions
Battn. H.Q. will move to The CUTTING,
CONTALMAISON (Pt. X.17.a Central.) from its
present position at 6.30.a.m. all reports
after that hour to The CUTTING.

3. A Collecting Station for prisoners will
be formed at X.28.b.2.6

4. Completion of relief of A and B Coys. to
be reported by runner to Battalion H.Q.

5. The Battn. will stand to arms in
fighting dress ¼ of an hour before
Zero on 17th inst. Each Coy. will
send a runner to Battalion H.Q.

6. O.C. A & B Coys. will each detail 1
platoon to be ready to carry bombs
& S.A.A. from CONTALMAISON VILLA to
BUTTERWORTH TRENCH.

Copy No. 1. O.C "A" Coy
      2. O.C "B" Coy
      3. O.C "C" Coy
      4. O.C "D" Coy.
      5. Lewis Gun Off.
      6. War Diary
      7. File.

George W. Duncan. Capt.,
Adjutant 8th Seaforth Hrs.

"A" Form.   Army Form C. 2121
MESSAGES AND SIGNALS.   No. of Message

Prefix	Code	m.	Words	Charge	This message is on a/c of:	Recd. at	m.
Office of Origin and Service Instructions			Sent		Service.	Date	
Priority			At	m.		From	
			To				
			By		(Signature of "Franking Officer.")	By	

TO D M

| Sender's Number. | Day of Month | In reply to Number | |
| * Br 832 | 17 | | AAA |

Send 1 Coy forwith to BUTTER
WORTH Trench between Junction with
LANCS Trench & MUNSTER ALLEY
aaa Guides for Company will
be at Junction ~~CONTALMAISON DE~~
~~ROAD~~ & GOURLEY TRENCH

From A R
Place
Time 12.45 p.

S E C R E T.　　　　　　　　　　　　　　　　COPY No. 2

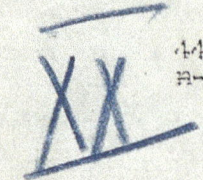

44TH INFANTRY BRIGADE OPERATION ORDER No.77.

Thursday, 17th August 1916.

1. The Company of 8th Seaforth Hrs. now in LOOP will relieve that portion of the 7th Cameron Hrs. in the captured portion of the German Switch as soon as possible.
   Guides from 7th Cameron Hrs. to report to O.C. Company 8th Seaforth Hrs. in the LOOP at once.

2. 1 Company of 9th Black Watch in BUTTERWORTH TRENCH to move into LOOP vacated by 8th Seaforth Hrs. and to be relived in BUTTERWORTH TRENCH by 1 Company 8th Seaforth Hrs. from GOURLAY TRENCH.
   This Company will also relieve portions of 9th Black Watch and 7th Cameron Hrs. in boyaux between GLOSTER ALLEY (inclusive) and GORDON ALLEY (exclusive).

3. Headquarters and 1 Company 8th Seaforth Hrs. to move to GOURLAY TRENCH and to be relieved by H.Qrs. and 2 Companies 9th Black Watch in CUTTING, CONTALMAISON.

4. On relief, 7th Cameron Hrs. will move
   　　Headquarters and 2 Companies to PEAKE WOOD.
   　　2 Companies to CONTALMAISON.

5. Before 6 a.m. on 18th the 2 Companies 8th Seaforths in GOURLAY TRENCH will relieve the two Coys. 9th Black Watch in Left of Section. Guides to be arranged between Battalions concerned. The 2 Coys 9th Black Watch thus relieved to move back to GOURLAY TRENCH.

6. Completion of relief and arrival in new positions to be reported by wire to Brigade Headquarters.

7. On completion of relief mentioned in para. 4, Brigade will be disposed as follows :-

   　　"A" Battalion 8th Seaforth Hrs.
   　　"B" Battalion 9th Black Watch.
   　　"C" Battalion 7th Cameron Hrs.
   　　"D" Battalion 8/10th Gordon Hrs.

Issued at 5.00 P.M.　　　　　　　　　　　　　　　　　　　　Major,
through signals.　　　　　　　　　　　Brigade Major 44th Inf. Bde.

DISTRIBUTION.

Copy No. 1. 9th Black Watch.
2. 8th Seaforth Hrs.
3. 9/10th Gordon Hrs.
4. 7th Cameron Hrs.
5. 44th M. G. Coy.
6. 44th T. M. Battery.
7. 15th Division.
8. 46th Inf. Bde.
9. 2nd Aust. Inf. Bde.
10. 15th Div. Arty.
11. 34th Div. Arty.
12. 73rd Field Coy. R.E.
13. 45th Field Ambce.
14. Bde. Signal Secn.
15. 9th Gordon Hrs. (Pioneers).
16. Staff Captain.
17. War Diary.
18. File.

SECRET. Operation Order by Copy No 6.
Lieut Col N.A. Thomson
Cmdg 8/Seaforth Highrs

XXI

Thursday 17th Aug 1916.

1. "B" Coy now in the LOOP will relieve that portion of 9th Cameron Highrs in the Captured portion of the GERMAN SWITCH as soon as possible. Guides for 9th Cam Highrs have been ordered to report to OC. "B" Coy in the Loop.

2. "B" Coy will be relieved by a company of 9th Black Watch now in BUTTERWORTH TRENCH.

3. "D" Coy now in GOURLAY TRENCH will relieve the above Coy of 9th Black Watch in BUTTERWORTH TRENCH.

4. "C" Coy will move to GOURLAY TRENCH to replace "D" Coy.

5. Battalion HQrs will move with "C" Coy to GOURLAY TRENCH.

6. "D" Coy will also relieve portions of 9th B.W. & 7th C.H. in Boyaux between GLOSTER ALLEY inclusive & GORDON ALLEY exclusive.

7. The above relief will be carried out at once.

8. Completion of relief to be reported to BATTN HQrs. (Junction GOURLAY TRENCH & YORKSHIRE ALLEY).

9. STRONG POINTS now held by the Battn will be relieved by 8/10th Gordon Highrs. On relief they will rejoin their Companies. George B Duncan
Capt & Adjt

"A" Form.
MESSAGES AND SIGNALS.
Army Form C. 2121.

Copy

XXII

TO: 8th Sea Highrs.

Day of Month: 14

AAA

As ordered by OC 7th Cams I attacked the Switch Elbow at 5.50pm. aaa The attack was successful in entering the enemy trench & we are making a block at S.1.d.5.8. aaa We have joined with the 7th Camerons at S.1.d.2.9 aaa. We are also deepening the trench at pt S.1.d.2.7 to S.1.d.4.7 & have got communication with Switch Elbow More reinforcements are necessary. AAA.

(248) A W Turnbull 2/Lieut

O.C. B. Co.

From: S.1.d.28
Place:
Time: 6.15pm.

"A" Form.
Army Form C. 2121.
MESSAGES AND SIGNALS.

Prefix....Code....m.	Words	Charge	This message is on a/c of:	Recd. at....m.
Office of Origin and Service Instructions.				Date
Copy	Sent			From
	At....m.		XXIII	
	To			By
	By		(Signature of "Franking Officer.")	

TO 8th Sea Highrs

Sender's Number. Day of Month. In reply to Number. **A A A**

Shelling heavy aaa. Am consolidating aaa
No counter attack yet aaa.

(Sd) A W Trumbull Lt
OC B Co

From 6·45pm.
Place
Time

"A" Form.
MESSAGES AND SIGNALS.
Army Form C. 2121.

TO 8th Sea Highrs

XXIV

I am holding the Quitch Elbow with connection with the Camerons on the N.W & H.L.I on the S.E.
1 platoon of "A" Coy (No 3) & Lt Fraser's platoon of "C" Coy have joined me.
There are no officers amongst the Camerons here. AAA There are no Germans visible — the Quitch Elbow line is full of dead —
I enclose identifications (No 179 & 22) found at 7pm at S.1.d.4.8
Heavy shelling continues.

(Sd) A W Trumbull Lieut
OC B Co

8.20pm

O.C. All Companies.   XXV D277

Ref map 1/5000 dated 1/8/16.

1. Munster Alley & the German Switch will be
occupied by four Companies as under:-
"B" Company from 4th Bde on our right (about
1.D.5.8) to where Bogan cuts German
Switch line (now called Cameron Trench) at
about 6.A.8.2 inclusive.
"C" Coy from Bogan at 6.A.8.2 (exclusive)
to 50 yds North West of Bogan about 6.a.7.4.
"A" Coy from 50 yds N.W. of Bogan about 6.A.7.4
to Australian Division on our left about
6.A.0.5.

2. At present the situation is as far as known
that "B" Coy with 1 platoon of A' occupy
German switch as far North West as about
1.b.0.1.
The Black Watch hold from the Australian
Division to about 6.A.7.4.
The line between the Black Watch & our "B"
Company is held by details of 4th Camerons.

3. The relief will be commenced by C Coy
at the earliest opportunity after 1 am.
A Coy will report relief complete to Battn
HQrs as soon as possible in order to allow
A Coy to carry out relief which will be
commenced as soon as orders that report
is received.

4. The 3 Companies holding the first line will find their own supports north of Butterworth Trench as ground permits.

5. D Coy will for the present remain in Butterworth Trench as a reserve - this Coy will eventually relieve B Coy under orders which will be issued later.

6. OC Companies must send in to Batt HQrs a report showing their dispositions as soon as possible giving rough sketch if possible.

7. Reports to GOURLAY TRENCH near its junction with YORKSHIRE ALLEY.

18/8/16.

George A Duncan.
Capt & Adj
8/Sea Highrs.

"A" Form.
MESSAGES AND SIGNALS.
Army Form C. 2121.

Prefix	Code	m.	Words	Charge	This message is on a/c of:	Recd. at	m.
Office of Origin and Service Instructions.			Sent			Date	
Corps			At ...... m. To ...... By		**XXVI** Service. (Signature of "Franking Officer")	From ...... By	

TO: 8th Sea Highrs

Sender's Number. | Day of Month. | In reply to Number. | **A A A**

Ref Op Order No. 16 aaa B Coy was moved up to Gloucester Sap at 3pm from BUTTERWORTH TRENCH by order of OC 7th Camerons as previously reported by me aaa.

At 5.50 pm B Coy captured the Switch Elbow + we have been there even since AAA

Only 59 remain in the Company AAA

We have established communication with H.L.I. & 7th Camerons who were holding the pnt captured & held yesterday morning AAA

Will relieve 7th Cams as soon as possible but the Germans are reported advancing

(Sgd) A W Turnbull 2/Lt.
OC B Coy.
8th Sea Highrs

From 12.5
Place
Time 18/7/16

The above may be forwarded as now corrected. (Z)

Censor. Signature of Addresser or person authorised to telegraph in his name.
* This line should be erased if not required.

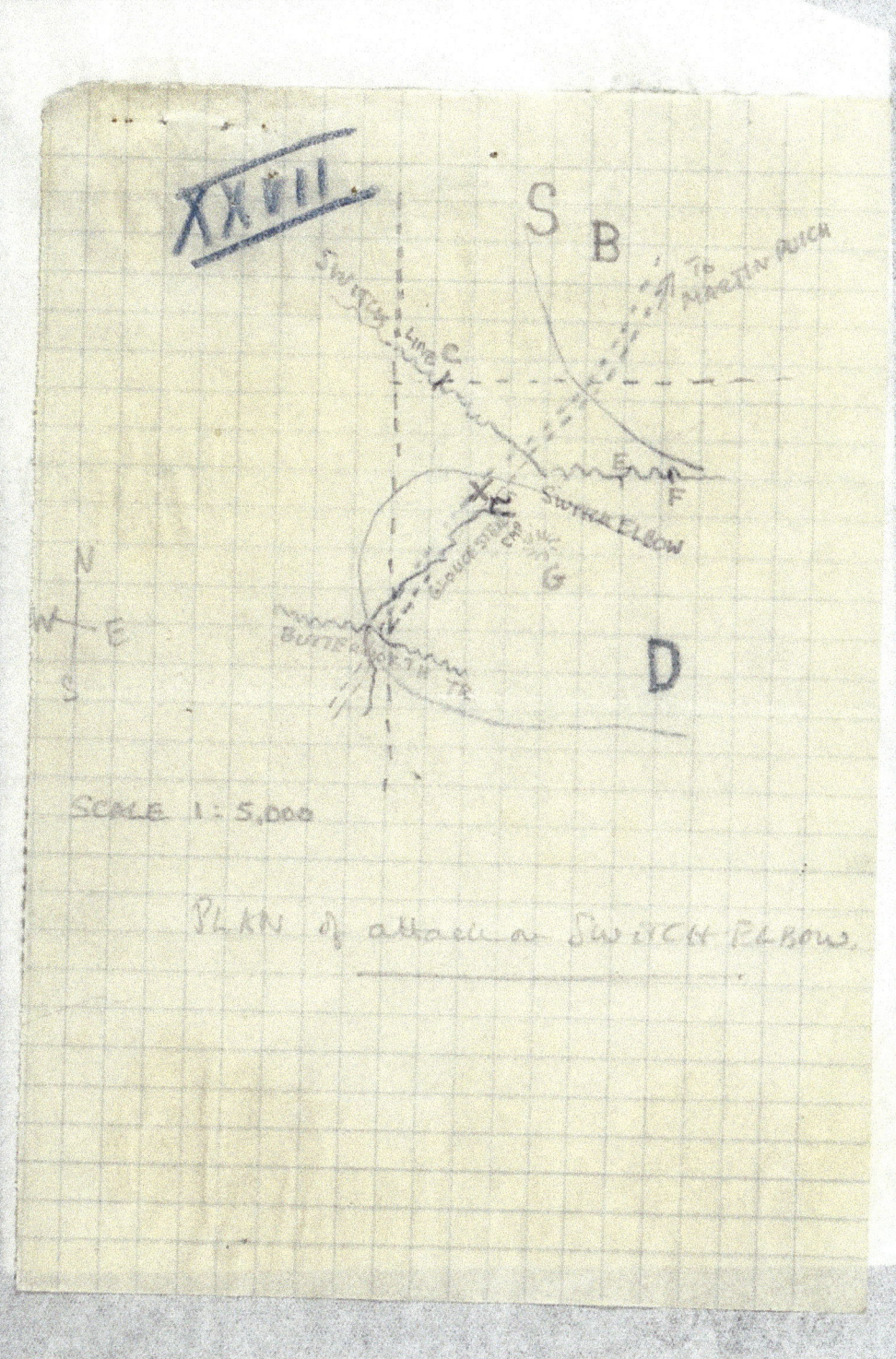

SCALE 1:5,000

PLAN of attack on SWITCH ELBOW.

Report on B Coy 8th Seaforth Highrs' Operations on
August 17. 1916.

At 4 pm B Coy was in BUTTERWORTH TRENCH & I was ordered by OC 7th Camerons to attack the German Switch line between the points C & E which had been retaken by the enemy. The Switch line up to Pt C was held by the 7th Camerons.

I arranged for a Stokes mortar to open a barrage on Pt F about 100 yds from the SWITCH ELBOW & to seize the trench between F & C at the same time. At 5.50 pm the barrage was established & one fighting 10 rushed the German line between B & C & the road & at the same time another 10 & a blocking party of 8 rushed the trench from the road to Pt F. All these parties left GLOUCESTER SAP at the same time & took the Germans by surprise. The Germans were all bombed & the trench immediately occupied. A permanent block was made at E & at temporary one at F & 24 dead bodies were found & 3 machine guns captured. A number of Germans who were hiding in adjacent shell holes fled towards MARTINPUICH & heavy casualties were caused to them by a Lewis Gun which I had placed near an old gun pit G. Connection was made with the 7th Camerons & the Right Brigade at once began to dig a trench to join the captured trench on the W side of the barricades.

Meanwhile we extended GLOUCESTER SAP up to the SWITCH LINE & consolidated the new line.

The Lewis gun was then moved up to the new line & its old place taken by a Vickers Gun of the 44th M.G.Coy.

Our casualties were 4 NCOs & men wounded during the actual seizure of the trenches.

A reserve of 25 men was kept in GLOUCESTER ALLEY in case of counter attack.

A.W. Hunthull 2/Lt
O.C. B Co
8th Bn Seaforth Highrs

21.8.16

XXVIII

S E C R E T.   Copy No. 2

Addendum No.2 to 44th Infantry Brigade Operation Order No.76.
_____

                                                    17-8-16.

1. Reference para 5.
        Time for bombardment on August 18th.
             8 A.M. to 10 A.M.
        instead of as therein stated.

2. Reference para 6.
        Five minutes intense bombardment will be 9-30 A.M.
        not 1-30 P.M.

3. No attempt is to be made by the Infantry to induce the
    enemy to expect an attack at 9-30 A.M.

Issued to   Major,
  Recipients of O.O.76.   Brigade Major,
  Through Signals.   44th Infantry Brigade.
      9-45 P.M.

S E C R E T.   44th Brigade.
                                                            B.M. 836

Addendum No.1 to 44th Inf. Bde. Operation Order No.78.

1. The Zero hour will be 2-45 p.m. at which hour the Smoke discharge will commence.

2. Watches will be synchronized at 1 p.m. on the 18th and not 8 a.m. as previously stated.

3. During the discharge of Smoke the line is to be thinly held. Lewis and Machine Guns to be active.

4. Zero time for this operation is not to be telephoned or wired.

                                              La Beck, Major,
                                              Brigade Major,
                                              44th Infantry Brigade.

17th August 1916.

To/
All recipients of 44th I.B. Operation Order No.78 d/17.8.16.

S E C R E T.   Copy No. 2

44th Infantry Brigade Operation Order No.76.

Reference :-   17-8-16.
15th Div. Map No.3.
   d/14-8-16. 1/5,000.

1. On the 18th instant the Right Division is attacking, among other objectives, the INTERMEDIATE LINE from the road in S.2.d. to S.2.0.7.4.

2. The 15th Division will co-operate by the discharge of smoke on the Front S.2.c.3.7. to MUNSTER ALLEY for 20 minutes.

3. The discharge will be at the rate of :-
    1 "P". bomb for 25 yards per 2 minutes.
    4 candles for 25 yards per 1 minute.
   Number of bombs issued to Front Line Battalion for 500 yards front :-
    10 bombs for each of twenty 25-yard portions of Front Line Trench = 200.
   Number of candles issued to Front Line Battalion for 500 yards front :-
    80 candles for each of twenty 25-yard portions of Front Line Trench = 1600.

4. 4" Stokes Mortars will also assist.
   One Section of 4th Coy. 5th Battn. Special Brigade R.E. will be placed at the disposal of the Brigade to assist in arranging the smoke barrage.

5. Special bombardments of the objectives and of the SWITCH LINE East of S.1.d.8.9. will take place :-
    August 17th) 10 A.M. to 2 P.M.
    August 18th)

6. "Chinese" (see below) attacks will be made during above periods.
    ZERO times as follows :-
    August 17th) 1-30 P.M.
    August 18th)
   There will be five minutes intense fire from minus 5 minutes to ZERO. At ZERO the fire will lift. It will jump back suddenly at ZERO plus 90 seconds.
   Dummies, bayonets etc. will be exposed to lead the enemy to expect an attack when the barrage lifts and so induce him to line his parapets before the barrage drops back.
   The line to be lightly held during these special bombardments to avoid loss from enemy counter-barrage which may be expected during last portion of each period.
   If no dummies have been received sandbags on pickets will be used instead.

7. The 200 smoke bombs and 1600 smoke candles will be issued under arrangements to be made by Brigade Bomb Officer.

8. Watches will be synchronized at 8 A.M. on the 18th, at which hour a representative of :-
    The Front Line Battalion.
    Section 4th Coy. 5th Battn., Special Bde. R.E.
    The Support Battalion.
   will report at Brigade Headquarters.

                           Major,
                         Brigade Major,   P. T. O.
                     44th Infantry Brigade.

Issued at 10-30 A.M.

44th Infantry Brigade Operation Order No.

DISTRIBUTION.

Copy No. 1. 9th Black Watch.
2. 8th Seaforth Hrs.
3. 8/10th Gordon Hrs.
4. 7th Cameron Hrs.
5. 44th M.G.Coy.
6. 44th T.M.Battery.
7. Bde.Bombing Officer.
8. Staff Captain.
9. O.C.Section 4th Coy.5th Battn.,Spl.Bde.R.E.
10. 15th Division.
11. War Diary.

"A" Form.			Army Form C. 2121
MESSAGES AND SIGNALS.			No. of Message

Prefix	Code	m.	Words	Charge	This message is on a/c of:	Recd. at	m.
Office of Origin and Service Instructions.						Date	
SECRET D.R			Sent At To By		XXIX Service. (Signature of "Franking Officer.")	From By	

TO   D M

Sender's Number.	Day of Month	In reply to Number	AAA
* Bm 846			

The ANZACS are attacking on our immediate Left this evening aaa The garrison of MUNSTER ALLEY from its junction with BUTTERWORTH Trench N.E. should be warned (in writing) to take cover behind Traverses etc at 8p.m at which hour our Artillery open aaa if they have to vacate the Trench they must not be allowed to go further back than to shell-holes in rear of MUNSTER ALLEY aaa acknowledge

From   A R
Place
Time   12.35 p.m

(Z)   EaB

SECRET.

15th. Div.
No.100/5 G.a.

44th. Inf. Bde.
34th. Div. Arty.

---

1. The 1st. Australian Division will be attacking tonight the enemy line from MUNSTER ALLEY X.6.a. 2.5 northwards. Time will be notified to you.

2. The General Officer Commanding has arranged that the 44th. Inf. Bde. is to vacate the block at the southern end of the enemy trench, and the 1st. Australian Division will order that their barrage is maintained not less than 150 yards from our trenches in X.6.a., heavy Artillery 200 yards.

The 44th. Infantry Brigade will assist in every possible way.

The 34th. Divisional Artillery will assist by firing on the area about X.6.a.5.8.

H. Kenox

Lieut. Colonel.
3.30 p.m.
18th. August 1916.   General Staff, 15th. Division.

Copy to :-
 III Corps.
 1st. Australian Division.

SECRET & Urgent.
44th I.B
B— 854   8th Seaforth H

Your information and
action as regards vacating block
mentioned in para 2 and assisting
in every possible way

J. a Beck, Major
Bde Major 44th Inf Bde

4.50 p.m.
18:8:16

"C" Form (Original).
MESSAGES AND SIGNALS.

Army Form C. 2123
No. of Message ....

Prefix SM Code HBR Words 43
Received From A.R By Clifford
Sent, or sent out At ...... m. To ...... By ......
Office Stamp

Charges to collect £ s. d.

Service Instructions. AR

XXX

Handed in at A R   Office 8.10 m.   Received 8.50 a.m.

TO   DM

*Sender's Number	Day of Month	In reply to Number	AAA
BM 888	19	—	

1st Div. have entered SWITCH redoubt M33D and found it unoccupied AAA They have established a post at NW corner of HIGH WOOD and cannot see any germans in northern portion of HIGH WOOD AAA They have placed a line of outposts along crest of ridge through S2D S3A S3C the anzacs on our left have reached railway X5B9.9 AAA CA occupies SWITCH up to S2C1.9 AAA

FROM   A R
PLACE & TIME   8 pm

"A" Form.
MESSAGES AND SIGNALS.
Army Form C. 2121.

Prefix .... Code .... m.	Words	Charge	This message is on a/c of:	Recd. at .... m.
Office of Origin and Service Instructions.				Date ....
Copy	Sent At ...... T ...... m. By		Service. (Signature of "Franking Officer.")	From ...... By ......

TO   A.R.

Sender's Number.	Day of Month.	In reply to Number.	
D 384	20		A A A

Patrol went out from MUNSTER ALLEY & reports that no signs of the enemy can be seen 400 yds from our front line AAA Patrol from west end of CAMERON TRENCH reports proceeded 200 yds from our front line & met no enemy AAA It reports the enemy lights were going up from outskirts of MARTIN PUICH AAA Patrol was stopped by our barrage AAA

Patrol from eastern portion of CAMERON TRENCH reports enemy line located about 700 yds from our front trench about outskirts of MARTIN PUICH AAA.

From JM
Place
Time 2/5 am.

SECRET OPERATION ORDER 16 Copy No. 5
by
Lt. Col. N. A. Thompson, D.S.O.
Commdg. 8th Batt~~XXXII~~ ~~Pabd. Hughes~~

Aug. 19th 1916

1. The Battn will be relieved by 8/10th Gordon Hrs. to-morrow.

2. Disposition of 8/10th Gordons will be as follows.

   "C" Coy. - 2 platoons in Cameron Trench between Swan Elbow & Gordon Alley.
   2 platoons in HIGHLAND TRENCH.

   "D" Coy - 1 platoon CAMERON TRENCH (west of GORDON ALLEY)
   1 platoon MUNSTER ALLEY.
   2 platoons BUTTERWORTH TRENCH (west of GORDON ALLEY)

   "A" Coy. 2 platoons BUTTERWORTH TRENCH (East of GORDON ALLEY)
   2 platoons - GOURLAY TRENCH

   "B" Coy - GOURLAY TRENCH.

3. Guides, as under, from 8th Seaforth Hrs. will be at junction of GOURLAY TRENCH and CONTAL MAISON ROAD, at 5.30 a.m. 20th inst.

   For "C" Coy. 8/10th Gordons - 4 guides from "B" Coy
   For "D" Coy.   "   "   - 1 Guide from "C" Coy
                               3 guides from "A" Coy
   For "A" Coy   "   "   - 2 guides from "D" Coy

3. On relief, companies of 8th Seaforth Hrs. will move to SCOTS REDOUBT - All movement to be by platoons at 5 mins interval

4. All Trench Stores will be handed over and receipts taken.

5. Completion of reliefs will be reported to Battn. H.Q.

                                       [signature] Capt.
                              Adjutant 8th Seaforth Hrs

Distribution
Copy No 1. OC A Coy
          2. OC B Coy
          3. O.C C Coy
          4. O.C D Coy
          5. War Diary
          6. File
          7. 8/10th Gordon Hrs.

SECRET.   Copy No. 2

44th Infantry Brigade Operation Order No.76.

19-8-16.

1. "B" Battalion, 8/10th Gordon Hrs., will relieve "A" Battalion, 8th Seaforth Hrs., on 20th August, under arrangements to be made between Officers Commanding Battalions concerned.

   On relief, which is to be completed by 7 A.M., 8th Seaforth Hrs., will move to SCOTS REDOUBT.

2. The 7th Cameron Hrs., "C" Battalion, will replace the 8/10th Gordons being in their turn replaced by 9th Black Watch, "D" Battalion.

3. Completion of relief and arrival in new positions to be reported by wire to Brigade Headquarters.

Issued Through Signals
at 6 P.M.

EaBeck.
Major,
Brigade Major,
44th Infantry Brigade.

Copy No. 1. 9th Black Watch.   6. 44th T.M.Battery.
         2. 8th Seaforth Hrs.   7. 15th Division.
         3. 8/10th Gordon Hrs.   8. 45th InfaBde.
         4. 7th Cameron Hrs.   9. War Diary.
         5. 44th M.G.Coy.   10. File.

~~SECRET~~

OPERATION - ORDER
N° 17.
~~XXX 847~~
Lieut. Col. N. A. Thomson, D.S.O,
Commdg. 8th (S) Battn. Seaforth Hghrs.

COPY N° 5

Aug. 21st 1916.

I   The Battn will relieve the 9th Black Watch in "C" Battalion as follows:-

"A" Coy 8th Seaforth Hrs. will relieve "C" Coy. 9th Black Watch with 1 platoon in Strong Point N.W. Corner of CONTALMAISON & 3 platoons in CONTALMAISON.

"B" Coy 8th Seaforth Hrs. will relieve "D" Coy. 9th Black Watch with 1 platoon in CUTTING, CONTALMAISON and 3 Platoons in CONTALMAISON.

"C" Coy 8th Seaforth Hrs. will relieve "A" Coy. 9th Black Watch in PEAKE WOOD.

"D" Coy 8th Seaforth Hrs. will relieve "B" Coy 9th Black Watch in PEAKE WOOD.

The two platoons of "A" Coy. + "B" Coy which are relieving the two strong points will be met by guides of 9th Black Watch at Bde. H.Q., CONTALMAISON at 5.20 a.m.

The remainder of the Battn. will move in the order A, B, C, & D Coys. - The first platoon of "B" Coy. to move from present position at 6 a.m.

All movements to be by platoons at 5 mins. interval.

2. Cookers will return to 1st Line Transport Lines.

3. Greatcoats will be taken to new positions.

4. All Gas Helmets will be worn as for Gas alert on moving off from present position.

5. Mess Boxes will be moved by fatigue parties under Coy. arrangements.

George W. Dunn, Capt. + Adj.
8th Seaforth Highlanders

Distribution.
Copy No 1. OC "A" Coy   4. OC "D" Coy
         2. OC "B" Coy   5. War Diary
         3. OC "C" Coy   6. File

Issued. Through Signals at 10.20 p.m.

SECRET.   Copy No. 2

44th Infantry Brigade Operation Order No. 79.

                                    Monday, 21st August, 1916.

1. "B" Battalion, 7th Cameron Hrs., will relieve "A" Battalion, 8/10th Gordon Hrs., on the morning of the 22nd August, under arrangements to be made between Officers Commanding Battalions concerned.

    On relief - which is to be completed by 7 A.M. - 8/10th Gordons will move to SCOTS REDOUBT.

2. 9th Black Watch will replace 7th Camerons, being in their turn replaced by 8th Seaforth Hrs.

3. Completion of relief and arrival in new positions to be reported by wire to Brigade H.Qrs.

                                    E A Beck, Major,
Issued through   Brigade Major,
    Signals.   44th Infantry Brigade.
    5-30 P.M.

Copies to :-
    No. 1. 9th Black Watch.   No. 7. 15th Divn.
        2. 8th Seaforth Hrs.   8. 45th Inf. Bde.
        3. 8/10th Gordon Hrs.   9. 2nd. Aust. I.B.
        4. 7th Cameron Hrs.   10. War Diary.
        5. 44th M.G. Coy.   11. File.
        6. 44th T.M. Battery.

SECRET. 44th Bde
~~XXXIV~~ B.M. 18/5
(15th Div 114/2 9a)

All Units 44th Inf Bde.

The following is a provisional programme of inter-brigade reliefs:—

46th Inf Bde relieve 44th Inf Bde in Left Section on 25th Aug

44th Inf Bde relieve 45th Inf Bde in Right Section on 31st August.

E A Beck Major,
Bde Major.
44th Inf Bde

23/8/16

SECRET

OPERATION ORDER No 18

by
Lieut. Col. N.A. Thomson, D.S.O.
Commdg. 8th Seaforth Highlanders

COPY No 6.

XXXV

Aug. 23rd 1916

1. The Battn. will relieve the 9th Black Watch as "B" Battn. to-morrow as under:-

"A" Coy will relieve "A" Coy. 9th Black Watch in CONTALMAISON.

"B" Coy. " " "B" Coy. " " " in CUTTING, CONTALMAISON

"C" Coy " . 1 platoon of "C" Coy and 2 platoons "D" Coy 9th Black Watch in trenches at N.W. corner of CONTALMAISON
1 platoon of "C" Coy. in CONTALMAISON VILLA.

"D" Coy. . 2 platoons of "C" Coy. & 2 platoons "D" Coy. 9th Black Watch in GOURLAY TRENCH.

"D" Coy. 8th Seaforth Hrs. will move from its present position at 2.30 a.m.

1 platoon of "C" Coy. which is proceeding to CONTALMAISON VILLA will be met by guide of 9th Black Watch at CONTALMAISON CUTTING at 2.45 a.m.

"A" & "B" Coys. will move to new positions commencing with "A" Coy. at 5.45 a.m.

Strong Pts. at present garrisoned by "A" & "B" Coys. will not move until relieved by 6/10th Gordon Hrs.

All movements to be by platoons at 5 mins. interval.

2. All Trench Stores will be handed over & receipts taken.

3. Arrival in new positions to be reported to Battn. H.Q.

4. Battn. H.Q. will move to THE CUTTING at 7.0. a.m.

Distribution
Copy No 1. O.C. "A" Coy.
2 O.C. "B" Coy.
3 O.C. "C" Coy.
4 O.C. "D" Coy.
5 War Diary.
6 File.

George W. Dunca, Capt.,
Adjutant 8th Seaforth Hrs.

Issued Through Signals at 8.25 p.m.

S E C R E T.   Copy No. 2

44th Infantry Brigade Operation Order No. 80.

23-8-16.

1. "B" Battalion, 9th Black Watch, will relieve "A" Battalion, 7th Cameron Hrs., on the morning of the 24th August under arrangements to be made between Officers Commanding Battalions concerned.

    On relief - which is to be completed by 8 A.M. - 7th Cameron Hrs. will move to SCOTS REDOUBT, becoming "D" Battalion.

2. 8th Seaforth Hrs. will replace 9th Black Watch, being in turn replaced by 8/10th Gordon Hrs., who become "C" Battn.

3. Completion of relief and arrival in new positions to be reported by wire to Brigade H.Qrs.

Issued Through   Major,
   Signals.   Brigade Major,
   2-30 P.M.   44th Infantru Brigade.

Copies to :-
No. 1. 9th Black Watch.   5. 44th M.G.Coy.   9. 44th Bde.Signals.
     2. 8th Seaforth Hrs.   6. 44th T.M.Bty.   10. 15th Div.
     3. 8/10th Gordons.   7. 45th Inf.Bde.   11. War Diary.
     4. 7th Camerons.   8. 5th Aust.I.B.   12. File.

S E C R E T.   44th Brigade B.M.28.

                                   (15th Div. No.114 (1)/2 G.b.)

All Units 44th Inf.Bde.

            WARNING ORDER.

1.   The 44th Infantry Brigade will not be relieved by the
     46th Infantry Brigade on the 25th August.

2.   The 46th Infantry Brigade will relieve the Left Brigade
     1st Division on the 27th instant.

3.   On the 28th instant an independant Brigade will be
     attached to the Division, and will relieve the 44th
     Infantry Brigade as soon as possible after arrival.

                                        Major,
                                    Brigade Major,
24-8-16.   44th Infantry Brigade.

"A" Form.   Army Form C. 2121.
MESSAGES AND SIGNALS.

Prefix	Code m.	Words	Charge	This message is on a/c of:	Recd. at m.
Office of Origin and Service Instructions. SECRET S.D.R		Sent At m. To By		✗✗✗✗ (Signature of "Franking Officer.")	Date From By

TO   8th Seaforth H

| Sender's Number. Bm 936 | Day of Month 25 | In reply to Number | AAA |

Ref this office Bm 935 of today's date aaa your Battn will be relieving A Battn tomorrow 26th Aug at the same time and will relieve that portion of 45th Inf Bde now holding the ANDERSON Trench from the present Right of this Bde Front to WELCH ALLEY (exclusive) at the same time, provided that the Division confirms the probable arrangements they have drawn up. Will you therefore please send the Officer Commanding the Coy which will be holding the your right to reconnoitre the new portion to be taken over & to ascertain what accommodation will be available

From
Place
Time 10.50 a.m.

(Z)   E a Beck Major

SECRET.   15th Div. No.114/2 G.b.

44th Inf.Bde.

Reference 15th Division No.114(1)/2 G.b. dated 23rd Aug.,1916.

The following will probably be the arrangements for the relief :-

(i) 26th August 1916.

44th Infantry Brigade to extend its right to WELCH ALLEY exclusive.

(ii) 27th August 1916.

(a) 46th Infantry Brigade to take over front from 1st Division from our present left to point (not yet notified) in S.3.d.

(b) 45th Infantry Brigade to put troops at disposal of 46th Infantry Brigade for relief of western portion (possibly to about S.2.d.7.2.) of this front. On completion of relief the 45th Infantry Brigade troops and front taken over by them will revert to 45th Infantry Brigade.

(c) The 103rd Infantry Brigade and 18th Northumberland Fusiliers (Pioneers), 34th Division, billet night of 27/28th at LABIEVILLE and come under orders of 15th Division.

(iii) 28th August 1916.

103rd Infantry Brigade and 18th Northumberland Fusiliers (Pioneers) move to Reserve Brigade area.

(iv) 29th August 1916.

103rd Infantry Brigade to relieve 44th Infantry Brigade in Left Section.

                                   (Sd) H. KNOX, Lieut.Colonel,
24th August, 1916.   General Staff, 15th Division.

                           (2.)   44th Brigade
                                                 B.M.935.
All Units 44th Inf.Bde.

For information.

Separate orders will be issued as regards paras (i) and (iv).

                                              Major,
                                          Brigade Major,
25-8-16.   44th Infantry Brigade.

"A" Form.   Army Form C. 2121.
MESSAGES AND SIGNALS.

Prefix	Code	m.	Words	Charge	This message is on a/c of:	Recd. at	m.
Office of Origin and Service Instructions.			Sent	XXXVIII		Date	
SECRET			At	m.	Service.	From	
S.D.R			To			By	
			By		(Signature of "Franking Officer.")		

TO: 9th Black Watch   8/10 Gordons
     8th Seaforth H.   7th Cameron H.

Sender's Number: BM 937   Day of Month: 23   In reply to Number: AAA

Warning Order

1. "B" Batt.n 8th Seaforth H. will relieve "A" B.n 9th Black Watch tomorrow morning under arrangements to be made between O.C. B.n concerned. Relief to be complete by 9 a.m.

2. "B" Batt.n will be replaced by 8/10 Gordon H. who in their turn will be replaced by 7th Cameron H. who become "C" Batt.n

3. On relief, 9th Black Watch will move to SCOTS REDOUBT becoming D Batt.n

From	AA	B
Place		
Time	4.20p—	

The above may be forwarded as now corrected.   (Z)   CarBeck

Censor.   Signature of Addresser or person authorised to telegraph in his name.

— Left Company "D"
— Left Company "C"
● Support Company "A"

XXXIX

8.G.H.
26/8/16

R M

S

D

150
155

36 31

1 N Co. 1 Owen
Shephend

Strong Point
1 N Co. 5 men

Strong Point
1 N Co. 5 men

Strong Point
1 N Co. 5 men

Strong Point
1 N Co. 5 men

Strong Point
1 N Co. 5 men

Strong Point

1 Platoon
2 Platoons

1 N Co. 1 Owen
Borley Post

Munster

1½ Platoons
1½ Platoons
1½ Platoons

Gordon Alley
Company Boundary
Cameron Trench
Sanderson Trench
Lewis Alley
Welsh Alley

Sussex Trench
Pirbie Post
6th
OG2
Gloster Alley
Butterworth Trench
Lancs Trench
Shetland Alley
Avenue
Battn Boundary
6th Avenue
Reids Alley
Welsh Alley

OG1
Gordon
Three Trees

● Remaining two Platoons of Support Coy & whole of Reserve Company in ___ Trench.   "B" Coy

S E C R E T.   Copy No. 2

44th Infantry Brigade Operation Order No. 81.

26-8-16.

1. "B" Battalion, 8th Seaforth Hrs. will relieve "A" Battn., 9th Black Watch, and that portion of the 45th Infantry Brigade now holding from the present Right of 9th Black Watch to WELCH ALLEY (exclusive) on the morning of 26th August, under arrangements to be made between Officers Commanding the Battalions concerned.

   On relief - which is to be completed by 9 A.M. - the 9th Black Watch will move to SCOTS REDOUBT, becoming "D" Battalion.

2. 8/10th Gordon Hrs. will replace 8th Seaforth Hrs., being in their turn replaced by 7th Cameron Hrs., who become "C" Battn.

3. On becoming "A" Battalion, 8th Seaforths will be disposed as follows :-
   3 companies in front line and supports.
   1 company in reserve in LANCASHIRE TRENCH and BUTTERWORTH TRENCH.
   Headquarters in GOURLAY TRENCH.

   The 8/10th Gordon Hrs. on becoming "B" Battalion will place two complete companies in GOURLAY TRENCH.

4. The guns of 45th M.G.Coy. in the area between WELCH ALLEY (exclusive) and H.L.I.TRENCH (inclusive) will be relieved by guns of the 44th M.G.Coy. by 9 A.M. 26th August.

5. Completion of relief and arrival in new positions to be reported by wire to Brigade Headquarters.

Issued Through
   Signals.
   6-0 A.M.

Major,
Brigade Major,
44th Infantry Brigade.

Copy No. 1. 9th Black Watch.
        2. 8th Seaforths.
        3. 8/10th Gordons.
        4. 7th Camerons.
        5. 44th M.G.Coy.
        6. 44th T.M.Battery.
        7. 45th Inf.Bde.
        8. 15th Div.
        9. 47th Div.Arty.
       10. 5th Aust.I.B.
       11. 44th Bde.Signals.
       12. Staff Captain.
       13. War Diary.
       14. File.

"A" Form.   Army Form C. 2121.
MESSAGES AND SIGNALS.

SECRET
S.D.R

XL1

Sender's Number.	Day of Month	In reply to Number	
Bm 957	26		AAA

With reference to Sketch Map shewing your dispositions and 44-1.B O.O. No 81 of todays date aaa The Brigade Commander directs that your 2 Platoons now in GOURLAY Trench be moved forward as soon as possible into LANCS Trench and 6th AVENUE in support of your right Company

From: 44
Place: 1.B
Time: 1.25 p.—

E. a Beck

SECRET

— DEFENCE SCHEME — Aug. 27th 191[6]

Lieut. Col. N.A. Thompson D.S.O.
Commdg. 8th Bn. Seaforth Highlanders

XLIII

1. The Battalion front extends from MUNSTER ALLEY (inclus.) to WELCH ALLEY (exclus.) There are three Coys. in the Front Line and each Coy. holds Strong Points in front of their Fire Trench. Front Line Coys. find their own supports.
   RIGHT COY. extends from WELCH ALLEY (exclus.) to H.L.I. ALLEY (inclus.) and holds 3 Strong Points about 100 yds. in front of SANDERSON TRENCH.
   CENTRE COY. extends from H.L.I Trench Alley. (exclus) to GORDON ALLEY (inclus)
   and holds 3 strong points at pts. S.1. b. 3. 1½
   S.1. b. ½. 2
   S.1. b. ½. 3½
   LEFT COY. extends from GORDON ALLEY (exclus.) to MUNSTER ALLEY (inclus.) and
   holds 2 strong points at pts. X.6.a. 9½. 5½
   X.6.a. 8. 7
   RESERVE COY. — 2 platoons in LANCS TRENCH between GORDON ALLEY and GLOSTER ALLEY and 2 platoons in 6th AVENUE between WELCH ALLEY and GLOSTER ALLEY.

2. Our Front Line and Strong Posts are to be held at all costs and denied to the enemy.
   Should the enemy gain a temporary footing in our front line, counter attacks will at once be organised and launched by the Senior Officer on the spot on his own initiative.

3. Commanders of platoons and Coys. in Support and Reserve Lines must constantly keep themselves informed as to the situation in front of them. All routes which would be used in the event of the Front Line having to be re-inforced, will at once be reconnoitred.

4. Officers Commanding Coys. must constantly keep Battn. H.Q. informed as to the situation in forward area. Under normal circumstances reports should be rendered once every two hours by day, and not less frequently than once every ¾ hours of an hour by night. This communication will be carried out by telephone when it exists and by visual or runner when wires are cut.

5. Bomb Stores as are per attached appendix "A".
   O.C. Coys. will at once tell off parties to carry bombs to the Front Line from the Support and Reserve Lines stores, in the case of emergency. O.C. Reserve Coy. will detail 2 platoons to carry from Battn. H.Q. store to stores in 6th AVENUE, GORDON ALLEY and LANCS. TRENCH. Headquarters personnel and cooks will carry from CONTALMAISON VILLA to Battn. H.Q. Store.
   The routes to all Bomb Stores should at once be reconnoitred — all ranks must know exactly where the nearest supply of bombs is.

6. ARTILLERY SUPPORT will be called for by the S.O.S. signal which will be given by the firing of one or two GREEN Very Lights or GREEN Rockets. A small store of GREEN VERY LIGHT cartridges & GREEN ROCKETS. will be kept at Battn. and Coy. Headquarters.

7. In the event of heavy hostile shelling or any indication of an enemy attack, all ranks will stand to arms.

George W. Duncan
Capt.
Adjutant 8th Bn. Seaforth High'rs

Appendix "A"

Bomb & S.A.A. Stores

Place	Establishment		Contents	
	Bombs	SAA	Bombs	SAA
Battn. H.Q. (near junction of GOURLAY TRENCH with YORKS ALLEY)	100	20	100	20
GORDON ALLEY (30' N. of O.G.2)	100	20	100	20
LANCS. TRENCH (100' E.T.N. of GORDON ALLEY)	25	10	25	10
HIGHLAND TRENCH (West of GORDON ALLEY)	25	10	25	10
HIGHLAND TRENCH (East of GORDON ALLEY)	25	10	25	10
Junction LANCS TRENCH with REID ALLEY			20	

PATROLS.

XLIV

(a) An officer and 3 men went out from CAMERON TRENCH from No.1 strong post at 10 P.M. last night. Guided by the CONTALMAISON - MARTINPUICH Road they reached the old German communication trench at S.1.b. central and worked northwards down it. At about 150 yards from BOTTOM TRENCH WEST they came upon a shell hole, scooped out to about 10 feet deep with what appeared to be a hole tunnelled into the side of it at the bottom. This shell hole was on the West side of the old communication trench and a few yards from it. The old communication trench itself was much flattened out and pitted with shell-holes. The patrol examined the shell-hole described above from the top only and listened for several minutes near it. They neither saw nor heard anything in this shell hole. The patrol then continued to the North and got within 50 yds of BOTTOM TRENCH WEST at a salient which the officer makes out to be at S.1.b.5.9½. Here they saw a enemy working party standing on the parapet digging. This party is estimated at about 15 men at the most. Very lights were being sent up by the enemy from one point only at this time - this point was about 200 yards East of the patrol (viz:- about the point where the old communication trench crosses BOTTOM TRENCH WEST). The patrol was observed by the enemy after watching for about two minutes and was fired at from the direction of the working party by rapid rifle fire. Very lights were then put up both from East and West - apparently from BOTTOM TRENCH - and also from a point about S.W. of the patrol and 20 yards from it. The patrol retired towards the South East and after retiring a few yards were further fired at by a machine gun from the West which was not at close range. They reached CAMERON TRENCH at 12-20 A.M.

(b) A patrol went out to investigate the old gun pits about X.6.a.9.9. These they found unoccupied with no signs of recent occupation.

"A" Form.　　Army Form C. 2121.
MESSAGES AND SIGNALS.　　No. of Message_____

Prefix____ Code____ m.	Words	Charge	This message is on a/c of:	Recd. at_____ m.
Office of Origin and Service Instructions.	Sent		**XLV**	Date_____
SECRET	At_____m.		Service.	From
S.D.R	To_____		(Signature of "Franking Officer.")	By
	By_____			

TO　DM

*Sender's Number.	Day of Month	In reply to Number	AAA
Bm 964	27		

News from G.H.Q. states aaa Bavarians pt HOHENZOLLERN are relieving Saxons opposite our front tonight and tomorrow night aaa Div directs that we receive them with indirect fire patrol constantly & do all we can to harrass their movements aaa the Artillery have been notified

From　AR
Place
Time　8 pm

The above may be forwarded as now corrected.　(Z)
Censor.　Signature of Addressor or person authorised to telegraph in his name.
* This line should be erased if not required.

which was in the hollow. (These are probably Snipers reported by patrol from Cameron Kopje).

The rails of railway in the open for about 50 yards South of pt S.1.6.9½ were observed to be broken by shell fire.

Patrol returned to Anderson Trench at 3 a.m.

(Sd) N.A. Thomson.
Lieut Colonel
Cmdg 8/Seaforth Hyhrs

28/8/16

S E C R E T. Copy No. 2

44th Infantry Brigade Operation Order No.82.
27-8-16.

1. "B" Battalion, 8/10th Gordon Hrs., will relieve "A" Battn., 8th Seaforth Hrs., on the morning of 28th August, under arrangements to be made between Officers Commanding Battalions concerned.

2. On relief - which is to be completed by 8 A.M. - the 8th Seaforth Hrs. will move to SCOTS REDOUBT, becoming "D" Battalion.

3. The 7th Cameron Hrs. will replace the 8/10th Gordon Hrs. as "B" Battalion, being in their turn replaced by 9th Black Watch as "C" Battalion.

4. Completion of relief and arrival in new positions will be reported by wire to Brigade Headquarters.

Issued Through
Signals.
2-30 P.M.
Copies to :-
SEE OVER.

E A Beck. Major,
Brigade Major,
44th Infantry Brigade.

Copy No. 1. 9th Black Watch.
2. 8th Seaforth Hrs.
3. 8/10th Gordons.
4. 7th Camerons.
5. 44th M.G.Coy.
6. 44th T.M.Battery.
7. 15th Div.
8. 45th Inf.Bde.
9. 5th Aust.I.B.
10. 47th Div.Arty.
11. 91st Fld.Coy.R.E.
12. Bde.Signal Secn:
13. War Diary.
14. File.

SECRET

OPERATION - ORDER No 19
by
Lieut. Col. N.A. Thomson, D.S.O,
Commdg. 8th (S) Battn. Seaforth Highlanders
— August 27th 1916.—

COPY N° 6

1. The Battalion will be relieved to-morrow, 28th Aug. by 8/10th GORDON HIGHLANDERS in the following order:—
   "D" Coy. 8th Seaforth Highrs. will be relieved by "B" Coy. 8/10 Gordon Hrs.
   "C" Coy.   "   "   "   "   "   "A" Coy.   "   "
   "A" Coy.   "   "   "   "   "   "D" Coy.   "   "
   "B" Coy.   "   "   "   "   "   "C" Coy.   "   "

   { Guides from 8th Seaforth Highrs. will be sent as follows:—
   2 Guides from "D" Coy. to guide 2 platoons of "B" Coy. 8/10 Gordon Hrs.
   which are taking over Strong Points to be at junction of GOURLAY TRENCH and CONTALMAISON ROAD at 3 a.m.

   { 1 Guide from "C" Coy. to guide 1 platoon of "A" Coy. 8/10th Gordon Hrs.
   which is taking over strong points to be at junction of GOURLAY TRENCH and CONTALMAISON ROAD at 3.5 a.m.

   { 2 Guides from "D" Coy. }   To be at Junction of GOURLAY TRENCH and
   { 3 Guides from "C" Coy. }   CONTALMAISON ROAD at 4.30 a.m. To guide
   { 4 Guides from "B" Coy. }   remaining platoons of "B" & "A" Coys
                                and "C" Coy. 8/10th GORDON HIGHLANDERS.

   4 Guides from "A" Coy to be at junction of YORKSHIRE ALLEY and GOURLAY TRENCH at 4.30 a.m. To guide "D" Coy. 8/10th Gordon Hrs.

   Route for "B" & "A" Coys. 8/10th GORDON Hrs. will be GORDON ALLEY and thence via shortest route.
   Route for "C" Coy. 8/10 GORDON HIGHRS. — GLOSTER ALLEY.
   Route for "D" Coy.   "   "   "   — YORKSHIRE ALLEY & WELCH ALLEY

2. On relief Coys. of 8th Seaforth Hrs. will move to SCOTS REDOUBT and take up positions previously occupied.
   All movement to be by platoons at 5 mins. interval.

3. All Trench stores will be handed over on relief and receipts taken.

4. 1 Limber for officers mess kit will be at the CUTTING, CONTALMAISON, at 5 a.m.

5. Completion of relief to be reported to Battn. H.Q.

George W Duncan
.... Capt.
Adjutant, 8th Seaforth Hrs.

Distribution
Copy N° 1. O.C "A" Coy
        2. O.C "B" Coy
        3. O.C "C" Coy
        4. O.C "D" Coy   6. War Diary
        5. O.C 8/10th Gordon Hrs. 7. File.

ISSUED THROUGH
SIGNALS ... 8.45 p.m

War Diary

XLVIII

S E C R E T.   Copy No. 2

44th Infantry Brigade Operation Order No.83.

Reference 15th Division   28-8-16.
Sketch maps Nos.5 & 5a,
dated 23-8-16.

1. On the 30th instant the 1st Division, in conjunction with operations elsewhere, will attack the German front line from S.10.b.9½.8. to where it strikes the western edge of HIGH WOOD - about S.3.d.9.8.
   Zero time for this attack will be intimated later.

2. There will be a deliberate bombardment by the Heavy Artillery commencing at 8 A.M. 29th August.
   From 1 hour 35 minutes before zero the intensity will increase, and the final 40 minutes will be intense.

3. At 2 P.M. on the 29th, and 10 A.M. on the 30th, provided the wind is favourable, the 15th Division will liberate smoke along their whole front. This will be done with "P" bombs only, for a period of 20 minutes.
   For this purpose "P" bombs at the rate of 20 for every 25 yards of the Brigade front (900 yards) will be issued, under arrangements to be made by the Brigade Bombing Officer.
   Half to be issued on 28th instant, the other half on 29th instant.

4. The 103rd Infantry Brigade will relieve the 44th Infantry Brigade on 30th August. The relief of the front and support battalions to be complete by 8 A.M. - Further orders will be issued.

5. O.C.8/10th Gordon Hrs. will make all arrangements for the liberating of smoke on the 29th instant, and for distributing half the number of smoke bombs issued at correct distances ready for use by the incoming battalion on the 30th instant.

5. For purposes of the smoke screen SANDERSON and CAMERON TRENCHES will be regarded as the front line.

                                                    F.a.Beck.
                                                    Major,
                                                    Brigade Major,
Issued Through   44th Infantry Brigade.
   Signals.
   11-0 A.M.

Copies to :-
       No. 1. 9th Black Watch.
           2. 8th Seaforth Hrs.
           3. 8/10th Gordon Hrs.
           4. 7th Cameron Hrs.
           5. 44th M.G.Coy.
           6. 44th T.M.Battery.
           7. 15th Division.
           8. 45th Inf.Bde.
           9. 103rd Inf.Bde.   13. Bde.Bombing Offcr.
          10. 7th Aust.Inf.Bde.   14. Staff Captain.
          11. 91st Field Coy.R.E.   15. War Diary.
          12. Left Group Div.Arty.   16. File.

SECRET

Copy No. 9

OPERATION ORDER No. 20

by
Lieut. Col. N. A. Thomson, D.S.O
Commdg. 8th (S) Battalion Seaforth Highlanders
August 29th 1916

Reference Map... ALBERT (Combined Sheet) 1/40,000

I. The Battalion will be relieved to-morrow, 30th Aug. 1916, by the 26th Battn. NORTHUMBERLAND FUSILIERS.

II. Companies will be relieved by corresponding Companies of the 26th Bn. NORTHUMBERLAND FUSILIERS.
Guides (1 per platoon) from 8th Seaforth Highlanders will be at Forked Roads (pt. F.3.b.3.5.) at 8.30 a.m. to-morrow, to guide incoming Coys. of 26th Bn. NORTHUMBERLAND FUSILIERS.

III. On Relief Coys. will move to Bivouac at Pt. W.29.d.8.4.
Route - Pt. F.3.b.35 - BECOURT WOOD.
All movements to be by platoons at 400 yds. interval.

IV. Cookers & Water carts will move from their present positions at 8.30 a.m.
Mess-boxes will be dumped at the old Battn. H.Q. at 9 a.m where mess cart will pick them up.
The Transport Officer will arrange that these vehicles move at an interval of not less than 50 yards.

V. Coys. will take with them their 50% picks and shovels.

VI. 1st Line Transport will remain in its present position

George W. Duncan
Capt;
Adjutant 8th Bn. Seaforth Highlanders.

Distribution
Copy No. 1. O.C. A Coy.
2. O.C. B Coy.
3. O.C. C Coy
4. O.C. D Coy
5. L.G.O.
6. Transport Officer
7. Quartermaster
8. O.C. 26th North. Fus.
9. War Diary
10. File

Issued Through
Signals. 4:30 p.m.

All Battns. 44th Inf.Bde.
    15th Division.
    103rd Inf.Bde.

<u>Addendum No.1 to 44th Infantry Brigade Operation Order No.84.</u>

Reference Table attached to 44th Infantry Brigade Operation Order No.84.-

Destination of 44th M.G.Company will be E.8.a.7.6. and not E.5.b.6.6. as therein stated.

28-8-16.

                      Major,
                Brigade Major,
        44th Infantry Brigade.

SECRET.   Copy No. 2

44th Infantry Brigade Operation Order No. 84.

Reference Map.   28-8-16.
ALBERT Combined Sheet 1/40000.

1. The 103rd Inf.Bde. will relieve the 44th Infantry Brigade in the Left Section III Corps on the 30th August in accordance with attached Table.
   Machine Guns and Light Trench Mortars will relieve on the 29th August.

2. Guides of "A" Battalion will proceed to Bivouac 25th North Fusrs. O.B.Line, Pt.X.26.d.2.6. on the evening of 29th instant.
   1 guide per platoon will be sent, and 1 guide from each of the strong points.
   The strong point garrisons of the incoming battalions will arrive at the Starting Point with the leading platoon. Guides for remaining battalions will meet their reliefs at Starting Point.

3. Machine Gun Company and T.M.Battery will relieve on 29th. The Nos.1 of each machine gun and each mortar will remain in the line until their services can be dispensed with.

4. All movements to be by platoons at not less than 400 yards interval.

5. During the relief all troops are to keep in the trenches.

6. The Nos.1 Lewis gunners of 25th Battn. North.Fusrs. will arrive at Brigade Headquarters, CONTALMAISON at 9 A.M. on 29th instant, where a guide will meet and conduct them to Headquarters "A" Battalion. They will remain with the Lewis Gun teams of "A" Battalion until the relief.

7. Units will bring out their 50% of picks and shovels to their bivouacs.

8. All trench stores will be collected at convenient places and handed over.

9. Battalions 1st Line Transport, with exception of water carts and cookers, remain in their present position.

10. Completion of reliefs will be reported by wire to Brigade Headquarters which, on completion of relief, will re-open at Pt.W.29.d.1.6.

Issued Through   F A Beck, Major,
  Signals.   Brigade Major,
  6-30 P.M.   44th Infantry Brigade.
                      DISTRIBUTION.
Copy No.-   9. 7th Aust.I.B.   16. Staff Capt.
1. 9th Black Watch.   10. 15th Div.   17. 47th Div.Arty.
2. 8th Seaforths.   11. 91st F.Coy.R.E.   18. III Corps H.A.
3. 8/10th Gordons.   12. Bde.Transport O.   19. 45th Fld.Amb.
4. 7th Camerons.   13. Bde.Supply Off.   20. War Diary.
5. 44th M.G.Coy.   14. No.2 Coy.Train.   21. File.
6. 44th T.M.Bty.   15. Bde.Signal Off.   22. Spare.
7. 45th Inf.Bde.

Table to accompany 44th Infantry Brigade Operation Order No.84. d/28-8-16.

Unit of 103rd Inf.Bde.	Unit of 44th Inf.Bde. to be relieved.	STARTING POINT. PLACE.	TIME. A.M.	Route for Units relieving.	Destination of Unit being relieved.
25th North.Fusrs.	"A" Battalion. 8/10th Gordons.	FRICOURT -	4-0	3 Co's GORDON ALLEY. Right Coy. WELCH ALLEY.	Bivouac at Pt. E.8.a.7.6.
24th North.Fusrs.	"B" Battalion. 7th Camerons.	CONTALMAISON Road at ROUND	5-0	Most convenient.	Bivouac at O.B.line Pt.X.26.d.2.6.
27th North.Fusrs.	"C" Battalion. 9th Black Watch.	WOOD.	7-0	- do -	Bivouac at Pt. E.5.b.6.5.
26th North.Fusrs.	"D" Battalion. 8th Seaforth Hrs.	(X.21.d.Central). Leading platoon of incoming battalion to arrive SCOTS REDOUBT.	9-0	- do -	Bivouac at Pt. W.29.d.8.4.
103rd M.G.Coy.	44th M.G.Coy.	To meet guides at H.Q. 44th M.G.Coy. CONTALMAISON 9 A.M. 29th inst.	9-0	- do -	Bivouac at Pt. E.5.b.6.6.
103rd T.M.Bty.	44th T.M.Battery.	To meet guides at Bde.H.Q., CONTALMAISON 29th inst.	9-30	- do -	- do -

S E C R E T.
==============

44th Brigade.
B.M. 983.

All Units 44th I. B.

WARNING ORDER.

    The Operations referred to in 44th Infantry Brigade Operation Order No. 83 dated 28th inst., to be undertaken by the 1st Division in conjunction with operations elsewhere are postponed for 48 hours.

29th August 1916.

                                                Major,
                                      Brigade Major,
                               44th Infantry Brigade.

8th(Service)Battalion,Seaforth Highlanders.

CASUALTIES FOR AUGUST,1916.

From 1st to 16th August -NIL.

Officers.

August.17th.2/Lieut.R.P.Smith.Wounded.
      18th.2/Lieut.J.H.Ross.   "
          2/Lieut.E.A.Maule.   "
      19th.2/Lieut.M.N.Ritchie."
      20th.   Nil
      21st.   "
      22nd.   "
      23rd.   "
      24th.   "
      25th.   "
      26th.2/Lieut.K.H.Grant.Killed.
          2/Lieut.J.Kirkwood.Wounded.
      27th.   Nil.
      28th.   "
      29th.   "
      30th.   "
      31st.   "

Total= 1.Killed.5.Wounded.

Other Ranks.

August.17th.10.Killed. 47.Wounded. 1.Missing.
      18th.18.Killed. 105.Wounded.   .
      19th. 6.Killed. 30.Wounded. Nil
      20th. Nil.   Nil.   Nil
      21st. "   1.Wounded.   "
      22.nd. "   Nil.   "
      23rd. "   1.Wounded.   "
      24th. "   4.Wounded.   "
      25th. "   1.Wounded.   .
      26th. 2.Killed. 18.Wounded. Nil.
      27th. Nil.   Nil.   "
      28th. "   2.Wounded. "
      29th. "   Nil.   "
      30th. "   "   "
      31st. "   "   "

Total =36.Killed.208.Wounded.1.Missing.

CONFIDENTIAL.

War Diary

of

8th (Service) Battalion Seaforth Highlanders.

From-1st September,1916. to 30th September,1916.

(Volume XV)

In the Field.
30-9-1916.

..........................Lt Colonel.
Comdg; 8th Bn. Seaforth Highlanders.

WAR DIARY
or
INTELLIGENCE SUMMARY.
(Erase heading not required.)

Army Form C. 2118.

Place	Date	Hour	Summary of Events and Information	Remarks and references to Appendices
M. ALBERT.				
N.24.D.8.4.	1/9/16		Companies had the use of Divisional shower baths at BECOURT WOOD. Kit inspections were carried out by Company Commanders. Batt of 80 other ranks joined the Battalion this day. Drainage received for Lt. M Rafferty Brigade	Appendix I
N.29.D.8.4.	2/9/16		Company training was carried out including training of Lewis Gunners, Signallers, &c. Nothing further to report.	Appendix
N.29.D.8.4.	3/9/16		All drafts which had joined the Battalion since 4th August were inspected by Brigadier General E.J. Marshall Commdg 144th Infantry Brigade. Nothing to report during the day.	
		10.30pm	About two hours the enemy fired 7 shells which landed they close to the Coys, at 11pm and then 7 shells landed in the same place & again at 11.30pm Another 7. No damage was done & no casualties occurred. No shells were fired after 11.30pm. Remainder of the night was quiet. Operation Ordr received from 144th Inf Bde.	Appendix II

WAR DIARY
or
INTELLIGENCE SUMMARY.
(Erase heading not required.)

Army Form C. 2118.

Place	Date	Hour	Summary of Events and Information	Remarks and references to Appendices
N.7.A & Sn.	4/9/16	5.45 Am	Battn. moved to SCOTS REDOUBT in accordance with Batt. Operation Order No 21.	Appendix III.
			Battn. took position in SCOTS REDOUBT by 8am.	
			Working party of 100 other ranks detailed for keeping Cable under 15th Divisional Signal Coy.	
			Nothing further to report.	
Scots Redoubt Sq.6	5/9/16		The Battalion moved from SCOTS REDOUBT relieved the 10th H.L.I. & 1 Coy of 4/5 KOSBs in accordance with Batt. O.O. No 22. - Relief was completed by 11.30 Am.	Appendix IV.
			Nothing further to report this day.	
			Bn. W.D. revised - this did not affect the Batt. directly.	Appendix V.
O.G.1.	6/9/16		No Operation of importance were carried out. Working parts of 50 men was supplied to work under Royal Engineers.	
			Warning Order received from 44th Brigade.	Appendix VI.
O.G.1.	7/9/16		Batt. this day relieved the 9th Camn. High in accordance with Batt. Operation Order No. 23. 9 mps. 44th Brigade B/M 133 dated 6th Septr. Relief was completed at 10 pm. D469 (Appendix VII) were issued to work during the night. - this was carried out by the Companies as ordered. Received & Copy to work report to 8 pm. 8/Septr. 1916 is attached. B/M 153 & App. 154 are also attached in connection with this work.—	Appendix VII. Appendix VIII.

T2134. Wt. W708—776. 500000. 4/15. Sir J. C. & S.

WAR DIARY
or
INTELLIGENCE SUMMARY.
(Erase heading not required.)

Army Form C. 2118.

Place	Date	Hour	Summary of Events and Information	Remarks and references to Appendices
QUARRY	7/9/16		14th I.B. Operation Order No 87 was received - Copies will not be in the Battn war diary covered by Every to 8th Sept. 1916.	Appendix IX
QUARRY	8/9/16		Military Situation with D49pr & 14th Brigade O.O. No 88 Thrombo attacks R.T. Burrison attacks the They been portion of Mont Wood from Zero time was 6pm - the 9th Black Watch cooperated - The Battalion tried to do all have set in any way affected by the operation except for some slight shells sent with L.M.G. guns.	Appendix X
		6pm.	14th Brigade B.M. 28 Messages Issued to Companies Intelligence Report to Every on 5th ind[?] is attached Mont was contained in accordance with D.489 (see appendix VIII) during the night - report on same does attached Nothing further to report a quiet night.	Appendix XI Appendix VII Appendix VIII
QUARRY	9/9/16		Intelligence Summary & from 9th inst is attached. In accordance with 14th Brigade O.O. No 89, Battalion O.O. No 24 was issued & all arrangements were made for the liberation of trench line from R.2 – R.Zero	Appendix XII Appendix XIV

T2134. Wt. W708—776. 500000. 4/15. Sir J. C. & S.

Army Form C. 2118.

WAR DIARY
or
INTELLIGENCE SUMMARY.
(Erase heading not required.)

Instructions regarding War Diaries and Intelligence Summaries are contained in F.S. Regs., Part II. and the Staff Manual respectively. Title pages will be prepared in manuscript.

Place	Date	Hour	Summary of Events and Information	Remarks and references to Appendices
Arory	3/9/15		Iron tree fired for 4.45 p.m. At 3 p.m. the code word "Scouts" was received from 9th Brigade denoting that the attack would not be operated.	
			The operation consequently did not affect the Battalion. During the night of 3/4th the Battalion was relieved by the 11th East Yorks in accordance with 9th Bde Brigade O.O. No 90 & Battalion C.O. No 25.	Appendix XVI
			A correction to 9th Bde Brigade O.O. No 90 two received, a correction was issued to Battn Operation Order No 25. O.C. No 91 was received from 9th Inf. Bde.	Appendix XVII Appendix XVIII
	10/9/15		Orders at 3 p.m. O.C. No 91 was received from 9th Inf. Bde.	
Oct 1st Over leaf			The relief in accordance with the above Order & Cancellation (Appendix XII & XVII) was completed at 5.45 A.M. & the Bn. handed over to the O.C. 4th East Yorks. The Battalion two on fatigue to OG.1 & OG.2 (vide Appendix XVII) by 9.30 A.M.	Appendix XIX Appendix IX
			Attached is Intelligence Summary to 7.30 p.m. 10th inst. Attached also is a tracing shewing position of Companies on OG.1 & OG.2. During the afternoon it was discovered that the Battn was in the 51st Divisional Area. Arrangements were made to move to OG.1 & OG.2 between the Bn District Boundary (roadway in Appendix IX) & the Colchester Martin Puich Road	

WAR DIARY
or
INTELLIGENCE SUMMARY.
(Erase heading not required.)

Army Form C. 2118.

Instructions regarding War Diaries and Intelligence Summaries are contained in F.S. Regs., Part II. and the Staff Manual respectively. Title pages will be prepared in manuscript.

Place	Date	Hour	Summary of Events and Information	Remarks and references to Appendices
O.G.1 & O.G.2	10/4/16		Nothing further to report this day. 3 parties of 10 men was supplied for carrying material for Gordon trench dug-out in O.G.1.	JM
O.G.1 & O.G.2	11/4/16		The Batln. moved to O.G.1 & O.G.2 when Brigadier Boundary & Colahaoon – Macketout went to 30am in shades up. There was no shell fire, but the whole Batln. were employed in digging in during the afternoon — Orders to Companies being invented numbers "1 Platoon of "B" Coy & 3 Platoons of "A" Coy were withdrawn to a new trench immediately north of the Carter Cockchafer. Work to be carried out in accordance with 4th Brigade Br. 197 & 31. – 4 officers & 150 men were employed to digging trench mentioned in Pars. 3 & 4 of BR. 31 & 1 officer & 50 men on trench mentioned in Pars. 3 & 4 parties were under Capt. A.N. TURNBULL & the work was completed by 3.30 A.M. – We had Lieut. Br. Le Mons. concealed his death by the enemy by a burst of gas shell, the only Casualty which occurred was Lieut. E.H. FRASER who was slightly gassed. JM	Appendix XXI. Appendix XXII.
O.G.1 & O.G.2	12/4/16	–	Nothing to report during the day - Working party of 3 officers & 150 men were employed in	

WAR DIARY
or
INTELLIGENCE SUMMARY.
(Erase heading not required.)

Army Form C. 2118.

Place	Date	Hour	Summary of Events and Information	Remarks and references to Appendices
			Accordance with 44th Brigade Bn. 31 (para 2). The posts were made. Capt. I.M. Jameson. The work was complete by 11 a.m.	Appendix XXIII
Bivouac X.24.c.	13/9/16	—	The Battn. was this day relieved by 6th Batt. Cameron Highlanders in accordance with 44th Bde. Brigade O.O. No. 93 & Batt. O.O. No. 25. Relief was complete by 10.40 a.m. On relief (together the Battalion moved back to bivouac at X.26.6. (immediately east of BECOURT WOOD).	Appendix XXIV Batt. O.O. No. 25 51A.S.E.
		10.30 p.m.	Warning Order received from 44th I.B.	Appendix XXV
X.26.6.	14/9/16	9.30 a.m.	Warning Order received to Companies. Further to report during the day.	
		4.15 p.m.	44th Bde. from the Battalion marched to CONTAI-MAISON & PEAKE WOOD in accordance with 44th Brigade O.O. 93 & Batt. O.O. 24. Batt. in bivouac by 10 p.m. Order messages received from 44th Brigade. Nothing further to report.	Appendix XXVI Appendix XXVII

WAR DIARY
or
INTELLIGENCE SUMMARY

Army Form C. 2118.

Place	Date	Hour	Summary of Events and Information	Remarks and references to Appendices
PEAKE (Wood)	15/9/16	6.20 A.M.	The 145th & 146th Infantry Brigade attacked the enemy trenches North & South West of Martinpuich – the 144th Infantry Brigade was in Reserve. Attached is the 15th Divisional Summary of Operations from 6am 15th inst. to 9am 16th inst. The Battalion remained in its present position all day & night.	Appendix XXVIII
PEAKE Wood	16/9/16		Situation no change as far as the Batt. was concerned.	
		3.30pm	Warning Order was received to be prepared to move into the area occupied by 15th Division as they were being relieved by the 1st Infantry Brigade.	
		6pm	The Batt. moved in accordance with Operation Order No 28 Herewith attached. Appendix 4. 115.Bty. They threw parties of Corp attacks. Nothing further to report.	Appendix XXIX / Appendix XXX
Contalmaison	17/9/16	9.40 am	Warning Order received from 144th I.B. & Corps Commander proceeded to reconnoitre the new front.	Appendix XXXI
		6 pm	In accordance with 144th Brigade Operation Order No 4 & Batt. O.O. No 29 the Battalion moved to relieve the 9th Bn 45th I.B. – Batt. Headquarters moved to junction of Welch Alley & O.B. Avenue – The relief was completed at 10pm.	Appendix XXXII

WAR DIARY
or
INTELLIGENCE SUMMARY.
(Erase heading not required.)

Army Form C. 2118.

Place	Date	Hour	Summary of Events and Information	Remarks and references to Appendices
Martin Puich	14/9/16		Attached is a sketch showing disposition of Companies. Before taking over the line a report was received stating that it was thought that the enemy had retired to the New line & that apart from a few snipers there were no Germans in front of the line. — Capt. G. Murray-Brown ordered to test this if possible.	Appendix XXIV
		10 pm	to reach the Kenora moving through N.26.A & B (see Appendix XXIII) — Col/Major Capt Murray reported that he had sent out a patrol to investigate the front his	
		11.25 pm	Col/Major Capt Murray reported that he had sent out a patrol to investigate the front his at 11.25 pm. This patrol returned reported that the Kenora was held by the enemy. The patrol attempted to enter the enemy trench but they has been forced to retire. One of the enemy had been shot dead by the patrol who in the act of throwing a bomb. Capt Murray also reports that the enemy had the wells steadily over the relief was carried.	Appx No XXIV
		11.30 pm	At this hour 144th Brigade Bn. 2/4 was received orders ordering certain strong points to be dug — & stating that the proposed offensive operation against the Kenora trench in N.27.A. & C (see Appendix XXIII) would not now take place.	App
Martin Puich	15/9/16	12.30 am	Orders were sent to "A" & "C" Companies to dig the strong points indicated in Bn. D.244 (Appendix XXIV) & this work was carried out during the night.	Appendix XXV

WAR DIARY or INTELLIGENCE SUMMARY

Army Form C. 2118.

Place	Date	Hour	Summary of Events and Information	Remarks and references to Appendices
Martin Puich	18/4/16		Nothing further to report during the day except that 3 prisoners of the 230th Regiment were captured by our post at 11.5 p.m. 24. C.2.2. One prisoner badly wounded & the two unwounded.	
		Noon	At noon a report was received from Capt Murray Commandt "A" Coy that the enemy were before themselves considerably, & he thought that if a white flag was sent up to him they might be induced to come in. — He thought there was a considerable number of them — Captain Rollo Staff Captain met Lt S.B. was sent up & orders were sent to Captain Murray to take all precautions to allow no more than 10 men unarmed to approach his post at one time hands up.	
		2.15 p.m.	At 2.15 p.m. Capt Rollo returned & reported that the Germans had disappeared & it was thought that they were afraid to come in in case they should be shot as deserters after the war. As soon as this message was received an intense artillery barrage was turned on to the trench where they had been known to be – this lasted from 2.45 p.m. to 3.15 p.m.	
		3.45 p.m.	At 3.45 p.m. orders were sent to Captain Murray to send out a strong patrol of 1 officer & 20 men to try & cut the enemy off in the trench running north & south	Appendix XXXVI

WAR DIARY
or
INTELLIGENCE SUMMARY

Army Form C. 2118.

Place	Date	Hour	Summary of Events and Information	Remarks and references to Appendices
MARTINPUICH	15/9/16		About 11.26 a.m. the message was sent by an officer of 9th Yorks Regt who was proceeding to reconnoitre the line –	
		(about) 12. 6 p.m.	message was received from Capt Murray that the message (Appendix XXVI) had arrived in a totally contrary (though illegible) sense – Verbal orders (?) were given to Capt Murray to send the patrol out – no details – (Appendix XXVI). The patrol went out but unfortunately one of the patrol threw a bomb into the entrance of a shell hole from which issued a number of the enemy who killed our patrol nearly without any casualties. The Bath. commenced to be relieved by the 9th Yorkshire Regt. in accordance with the Bath. Operation Order No. 30.	Appendix XXVI
		4.4. S.B.	Operation Order No. 95 (Bath. Operation Order No. 30). The relief was complete at 11.40 pm. – On relief the Battalion moved back to trenches in M 29 d Central (just East of ALBERT). Owing the frost Butchery to the Rendez great difficulty was experienced in maintaining communication with first line Companies from Bath. H.Qrs. – Telephone communication was bad & owing to the very wet weather it took runner a long time to reach the Companies. – Bath. headquarters was too far back & it was impossible to get	

WAR DIARY or INTELLIGENCE SUMMARY

Army Form C. 2118.

Place	Date	Hour	Summary of Events and Information	Remarks and references to Appendices
MARTINPUICH	18/4/16		Other Ranks to Companies - New Headquarters now taken over the previous left for Officers LH.	
ALBERT	19/4/16	11 am	The Battalion marched to LAVIEVILLE in accordance with 44th Brigade OO No 96 & Batt. OO No 31 - Battalion arriving in billets at 1.15pm. -	Appendix XXVIII
LAVIEVILLE		1.15pm	All Officers who have been left behind at the Reinforcement Camp while the Battalion was in the line rejoined the Battalion this day.	
LAVIEVILLE	20/4/16		The Battalion marched from LAVIEVILLE to FRAMILLERS in accordance with 44th Brigade Operation Order No 97 & Batt. Operation Order No 32 - Both in billets by 12 noon.	Appendix XXIX
FRAMILLERS		12 noon	Nothing further to report -	
FRAMILLERS	21/4/16		The day was devoted to general cleaning up. Kit-inspection by Company Commanders. Working parties of 50 men found by Companies to Bde Bombing Ground.	Appendix XL
FRAMILLERS	22/4/16		Training was carried on as per attached programme - the Battalion had the use of the Baths also - Working party of 50 men found as yesterday.	Appendix XL
FRAMILLERS	23/4/16		Training was carried on as per attached programme. Working party of 50 men found as yesterday for Bde Bombing Ground.	Appendix VI

Army Form C. 2118.

WAR DIARY
or
INTELLIGENCE SUMMARY.
(Erase heading not required.)

Instructions regarding War Diaries and Intelligence Summaries are contained in F. S. Regs., Part II. and the Staff Manual respectively. Title pages will be prepared in manuscript.

Place	Date	Hour	Summary of Events and Information	Remarks and references to Appendices
FRANVILLERS	24/4/16		Church parades were held during the morning. Nothing further to report.	
FRANVILLERS	25/4/16		Training carried out as per attached programme.	Appendix XLII
FRANVILLERS	26/4/16		Training carried on as per attached programme.	Appendix XLIII
FRANVILLERS	27/4/16		The Battalion route marched as per attached programme via RIBEMONT, HEILLY, BONNAY, FRANVILLERS. Cookers were not attached. Tea & dinner were served on return to billets at 1.30pm.	Appendix XLIV
FRANVILLERS	28/4/16		Training carried on as per attached programme. An officer personally attended a lecture to the New Boys Regiment at Divn Gas School. A Superintendent Physical Training 4th Army lectured to all officers & platoon sergeants.	Appendix XLV. Appendix XLVI
FRANVILLERS	29/4/16		Owing to the inclement weather little training was done this day. Lectures were given by Company & Platoon Commanders on Trench routine, observation, Listening posts, R. A party of 50 other ranks proceeded as part of a permanent party to ALBERT	

T2134. Wt. W708—776. 500000. 4/15. Sir J. C. & S.

WAR DIARY
or
INTELLIGENCE SUMMARY.
(Erase heading not required.)

Army Form C. 2118.

Place	Date	Hour	Summary of Events and Information	Remarks and references to Appendices
FRANVILLERS	29/9/16		At work under CRE III Corps.	Appendix XLVII
FRANVILLERS	30/9/16		Permanent Works, parts of 4 other ranks proceeded to ST GRATIEN for work under the 249th A.T. Coy R.E. Training was carried on in accordance with attached programme.	Appendix XLVIII Appendix XLIX
			Appendix I shows list of casualties for Sept 1916. Total being — 11 Offrs wounded 12 Other Ranks killed 85 " " wounded	
			Appendix II shows Reinforcements which joined the Battalion during the month.	

SECRET

III. OPERATION ORDER No. 21.

by
Lieut. Col. N. A. Thomson D.S.O,
Commdg. 8th (S) Battn. Seaforth Highlanders.

3rd Sept. 1916.

1. The Battn. will move to SCOTS REDOUBT, to-morrow as follows:-
   STARTING POINT ... Battalion Guard Tent.
   TIME .... 5.45 a.m.
   ORDER OF MARCH ... "A", "B", "C" & "D" Coys., Headquarters,
                       Lewis Gun Detachment.

   Route ... ALBERT - BECOURT - LOZENGE Wood Road.
   All movements to be by platoons at 200 yds. interval.

   ~

2. Cookers & Water-carts will accompany the Battn.
   Mess-Boxes will be collected at 6.30 a.m.

   ~

3. Packs & Officer's Valises will be stacked in Camp by Coys.
   The Quartermaster will arrange that these are taken back
   to Quartermaster's Stores.

   ~

4. All ranks will move off from present position in "Fighting Order"
   "plus greatcoats"

   ~

5. Advance party of 1 N.C.O. per Coy. & 1 for Headquarters, will
   parade at Battn. H.Q. on bicycles under 2/Lieut. J.H. Ross
   at 5 a.m.

   These N.C.O's will meet their respective Coys. on main
   FRICOURT - CONTALMAISON Road & guide them to their
   positions.

   ~

6. ~~Completion of~~ Arrival in new positions to be reported to Battn. H.Q.

   ~

George W Duncan.
Captain.
Adjutant 8th Seaforth Highrs.

Distribution.
Copy No 1. O.C. "A" Coy.
       2. O.C. "B" Coy.
       3. O.C. "C" Coy.
       4. O.C. "D" Coy.
       5. L.G.O
       6. 2/Lieut. J.H. Ross.
       7. Transport Officer
       8. Quartermaster
       9. War Diary.
      10. File.

Issued Battalion Orders at 5.30 p.m.

SECRET   Operation Order No 22.   Copy No 8
                              by
                  Lieut. Col. A. Thomson. D.S.O.
                  Commdg. 8th Battn. Seaforth Highrs
                          Sept. 4th 1916

1. The Battalion will relieve 3 Companies 10th/11th H.L.I. and 1 Company 7th/8th K.O.S.B's in Brigade Support in the Right Section tomorrow.
   "A" Coy will relieve "A" Coy 10th/11th H.L.I. in O.G.I.
   "B" Coy will relieve "B" Coy 10th/11th H.L.I. in O.G.I.
   "C" Coy will relieve "D" Coy 10th/11th H.L.I. in O.G.I.
   "D" Coy will relieve will relieve one Company K.O.S.B's 7th/8th, in O.G.I with one platoon at the west side of BAZENTIN - LE PETIT WOOD.

2. Companies will move off from present position in the following order:-
   "A", "C", "B", "D" Companies, Headquarters Lewis Gun Detachment.
   The first platoon of "A" Coy to move at 9 a.m.
   Route:- CONTALMAISON, THE CUTTING, to N.W. Corner of MAMETZ WOOD, where guides (4 per Company) from 10th/11th H.L.I. and 7th/8th K.O.S.B's) will meet them at 10.0. a.m.
   All movements to be by platoons at not less than 400 yards interval.
   It is most important that troops should not crowd together and that no blocks should occur.

3. The Lewis Gun Officer will detail 4 Lewis Guns from Headquarters Detachment to proceed with the platoon of "D" Coy which is to be at west side of BAZENTIN LE PETIT WOOD.

4. Advanced parties of 1 N.C.O. per Company and one for Headquarters will proceed to take over Trench Stores at 8.0. a.m. tomorrow –
   Receipts will be given, and lists of Trench Stores taken over rendered to Battalion Headquarters by 6. p.m. on 4th Sept.

5. The Transport Officer will detail 2 limbers to be at SCOTS REDOUBT at 9-30. a.m. to transport disselves.
   All mess boxes will be dumped at Old Battalion Headquarters by 9-30 a.m. Mess Cart will be there at that time.
   These vehicles will not proceed past the North West Corner of MAMETZ WOOD and will move at 50 yards interval.
   Cookers and Water Carts will return to 1st Line Transport.

6. Greatcoats will be carried by all ranks.

7. Completion of relief to be reported by runner to New Battalion Headqrs which is situated at Point S. 13. b. 2. 9.

                               George W. Duncan.
                                        Captain
                         Adjt. 8th Battn Seaforth Highlanders.

Distribution:- Copy No 1 ... "A" Coy.
                        2 ... "B" Coy.
                        3 ... "C" Coy.
                        4 ... "D" Coy.
                        5 ... L.G.O.
                        6 ... Transport Officer.
                        7 ... Quartermaster.
                        8 ... War Diary.
                        9 ... File.

SECRET.   Operation Order No. 23.   Copy No. 10
           by Lieut Col N.A. Thomson D.S.O.
           Cmdg 8th Seaforth Highrs.
                                              3rd Septr. 1916.
Ref. 15th Div. Map No 6A & 6B 1/5000 dated 2/9/16.

1. The Battn. will relieve the 7th Cameron Highrs. today as follows:-
    "A" Company will relieve "A" Coy 7th Cameron Highrs. in MILL STREET.
    "C" Company "   "   "C" Coy "   "   "   in THE QUARRY.
    "B" Company "   "   "B" Coy "   "   "   in the front line from
            pt. S.2.c.3.2½ to KERRY ALLEY (inclusive) & will also take
            over front line from KERRY ALLEY to the base of BETHELL SAP
            (exclusive) from 9th Black Watch.
    "D" Company will relieve "D" Company 7th Cam Highrs with 3 platoons
            in new trench which runs from pt S.2.d.5.8½ to
            pt. S.2.d.8.8. & 1 platoon in 6th Avenue East.
    "A" & "C" Companies will relieve during the afternoon – the first
    platoon of "A" Company moving from present position at 4.p.m. –
    remaining platoons of "A" Coy & "C" Coy will follow by platoons
    at 5 minutes interval.
    Guides from 7th Cameron Highrs will meet platoons of "A" & "C"
    Companies at the CEMETARY.
    "B" & "D" Companies will move off from present position by platoons
    at 5 minutes interval – the first platoon of "B" Coy to arrive
    at the CEMETARY at 8p.m. – Guides from 7th Cameron Highrs will
    meet platoons of "B" & "D" Companies at the CEMETARY.

2. OC. "D" Company will detail 1 guide to proceed with "C" Company
   8th Seaforth Highrs – this guide will conduct a platoon of "C"
   Company 7th Cameron Highrs which is taking over Strong point
   from "D" Company 8th Seaforth Highrs in BAZENTIN-LE-PETIT Wood.

3. The Lewis Gun Officer will detail 2 Lewis Guns & teams from H.Q.
   detachment to proceed with "B" Coy in addition to the Coy gun.

4. Omit OC. "C" Coy will take over guard of 1 NCO. & 2 men on Brigade
   Advanced Bomb Store in the Quarry.

5. Trench Stores will be taken over by "B" & "D" Coys at 3p.m. today "A" & "C" Companies will take over Trench Stores on relief. Receipts to be rendered to Battn H.Qrs by 12 noon 8th inst.

6. Greatcoats will be taken to the ration dump today & returned to Quartermasters' Stores.

7. Battalion Headquarters will move to new position in the Trams at 8.30pm.

8. Completion of relief to be reported to Battn Headquarters by wire or runner.

George W. Duncan
Captain
Adjutant 8th Battn Seaforth Highlanders.

Distribution Copy No 1. O.C. "A" Coy.
" " 2. O.C. "B" Coy.
" " 3. O.C. "C" Coy.
" " 4. O.C. "D" Coy.
" " 5. O.C. 7th Cameron High.
" " 6. O.C. 9th Black Watch.
" " 7. Lewis Gun Officer.
" " 8. War Diary
" " 9. File.

Issued through Signals at 1.35pm.

3. All the above parties will work for not less than 4 hours.
4. O.C. Companies will report by 5-30 a.m. tomorrow the amount of work done.
5. The urgency of this work is to be impressed upon all ranks.

George W. Duncan.
Captain
Adjutant 8th Batt. Seaforth Highlanders

17-9-16

SECRET   D.459

Officers Commanding, All Companies.

Ref. 15th Div. Map. No 6ᴬ & 6ᴮ. 1/5000 dated 2/9/16

1 Work will be carried out tonight as follows :—

(a) A new sap running due North from junction of KERRY ALLEY and CLARK'S TRENCH is to be continued to the "150" Contour line at Pt. S.3.a.5.4. and deepened to a depth of 5 feet. It will then be T headed at that Point.

(b) A new sap running N.E from junction of JUTLAND ALLEY and SWANSEA TRENCH is to be continued to the "150" Contour line at Pt. S.3.a.0.3½. and deepened to a depth of 5. feet.
It will then be T. headed at that Point.

(c) The heads of the two saps mentioned in (a) & (b) will be joined up by a trench 4'- 6" deep forming a new line, which will follow the line of the "150" Contour line.
This new line is being taped out by the R.E tonight at dark.

(d) The present front line from Pt. S.2.b.3.2½ to base of BETHELL SAP will be deepened, revetted and firestepped.

(e) The new trench running from S.2.d.5.8½ to Pt. S.2.d.8.8. will be continued Eastwards to the second Y in KERRY ALLEY

2 (a) Work stated in Para 1.(a) will be carried out by 1 officer & 50 men of "A" Coy.
Work stated in Para 1.(b) will be carried out by 1 officer & 50 men of "C" Coy.
When these saps are completed these parties will commence working Westwards and Eastwards respectively to form new line stated in Para 1.(c).
All work stated in Para 1.(a) (b) & (c) will be under an Officer to be detailed by O.C. "A" Coy. The officers proceeding with these parties will report at Battn. Headquarters at 9-15 p.m.
"A" Coy's party will move off from present position at 10-15 p.m.
"C" Coy's party will move off from present Position at 10-30 p.m.
A Covering Party of 1 officer & 20 men for these parties will be found by O.C. "B" Coy.
The requisite number of tools will be carried.

(b) Work stated in Para 1.(d) will be carried out by "B" Coy. who are in occupation of that part of the line.
A Party of 1 N.C.O. & 20 men will be detailed by O.C. "C" Coy to assist "B" Coy in this work - This Party will report to O.C. "B" Coy at 10-15 p.m.

(c) Work stated in Para 1.(e) will be carried out by "D" Coy.

(Cont'd)

SECRET.
S.D.R.

44. I.B.
B.M. 154.

~~7th Cameron Hdrs~~
~~8/10. Gordon Hdrs~~
8th Seaforth Hdrs

Reference verbal instructions regarding work given you today, the Durham Pioneers will be digging extension of JUTLAND ALLEY forward.
The extension of KERRY ALLEY requires 25 yards more to be dug up to an old enemy Trench which will be used & will form part of the new front-line.
The R.E. will tape out tonight at dusk.

(a) From head of KERRY extension to west arm of BETHELL SAP.

(b) From head of KERRY extension to head of JUTLAND extension.

(c) From head of JUTLAND extension to head of SOMME extension & thence to 'CUTTING' S.26.4.5.

The work from KERRY ALLEY extension to left arm of BETHELL SAP will be worked on by a party of 150 from 7th Cameron Highlanders and dug to a depth of 4 feet. The tape for this portion will be laid ready for work to commence at 10 p.m. On completion of this task the party will rejoin its Battalion in Brigade Support.
The work from KERRY extension westwards will be done by 8th Seaforth Hdrs, that portion between JUTLAND ALLEY extension and the CUTTING being taken over by 8/10 Gordon Hdrs tomorrow & to be completed by them on night 8/9th Sept.
The precautions of putting out covering parties should not be neglected.
The 15th Division are arranging their Artillery programme accordingly.

Rec'd
8 p.m.

9.0 p.m.
9 p.m.

7.9.16.

E.A.Beck, Major
Brigade Major
44th Inf. Bde.

SECRET

O.C. All Companies.
Lewis Gun Officer.

D 494.

Reference III Corps (I) Map - Sheet 13.B. 1/10000.

1. (a) 1st Division will attack the West Portion of HIGH WOOD on 8th Sept. their infantry advancing to the assault at Zero under a barrage which will lift at Zero plus 1½ mins.
   (b) The 44th Infantry Brigade will cooperate by seizing the German trench which runs from pt. S.3.b.8.3 to pt. S.3.b.6.5.
   (c) Southern End of BETHELL SAP will be cleared by pioneers of 50th Division on night of 7/8th Sept.

2. 9th Black Watch will carry out this operation advancing under the barrage at the same time as the 1st Division. At least two companies will be kept available in & near BETHELL SAP for this purpose.

3. A "jumping off" trench will be dug by 9th Black Watch from Eastern arm of BETHELL SAP to the S.E., parallel with the Road & not more than 20 yds from it. Work to be completed by 5 a.m. 8.9.16.

4. 15th Divn Medium T.M's (2 guns) & 44th L.T.M. Battery (2 guns) will cooperate as follows:-
   15th Divn Medium T.M's - 1 gun to deal with suspected M.G about S.3.b.9.2½
                          1 gun about S.3.b.2.8.
   44th L.T.M. Battery - Both guns assist in barrage, thereafter as occasion demands. Special attention to be paid to M.G's.

5. Brigade Signal Officer will arrange for a Brigade Visual Signalling Post to be established at about S.9.a.9½.2. (ARGYLL TRENCH) - O.C. 9th B.W. will be responsible for maintaining communication from the post to this post.

6. At Zero hour Companies of 8th Seaforth H'l'rs will stand to in fighting dress prepared to carry out any instructions they may receive, at shortest notice.

7. Zero time & arrangements for synchronization of watches will be notified later.

George W. Duncan.
Captain
Adjutant 8th Battn Seaforth Highlanders.

7th Sept. 1916.

U R G E N T.

XXII

44th Brigade B.M.31.

O.C. 8th Seaforth Hrs.
    8/10th Gordon Hrs.
    7th Cameron Hrs.
    74th Fld.Coy.R.E.

WORK FOR NIGHT 11/12th SEPTEMBER.

1. Para 4 of 44th Brigade B.M.197 of 10-9-16 is cancelled.

2. **7th Cameron Hrs.**

   (a) Improve "A" trench to 4-ft deep and $1\frac{1}{2}$-ft broad at the bottom.
   (b) Improve boyaux leading to "A" trench.
   (c) Improve boyaux leading to "B" trench.
   (d) Clear H.L.I. trench.

3. **8th Seaforth Hrs.**

   (a) Dig a trench from the western end of "B" trench (about Pt.S.1.b.6.3.) to join the extension of SHETLAND ALLEY about Pt.S.1.b.3.$4\frac{1}{2}$. Length about 150 yards 4-ft deep $1\frac{1}{2}$-ft broad at bottom.

   (b) Improve "B" trench to 4-ft deep and $1\frac{1}{2}$-ft broad at the bottom.

11-9-16.

Brigade Major,
44th Infantry Brigade.

44th Brigade.
B.M.F1.

WORK for Night 12th/13th Septr.

7th Cameron Hrs.

    (a) Improve "B" trench to 4 feet deep and 1½ feet broad at bottom.

    (b) Clear LANCS. TRENCH between H.L.I. ALLEY and WELCH ALLEY.

    (c) Improve deviation to Eastern boyau to trench "B"; (the rest of this boyau need not be improved by us as Pioneers are going to take it over). All that is required is to keep it in sufficiently good repair to admit of traffic to "B" trench.

8th Seaforth Hrs.

    Dig boyau from SWITCH ELBOW through "A" trench to join "B" trench. About 250 yards.

9th Black Watch.

    Dig "C" trench from about Pt. S.2.a.4.2. to about S.1.b.6.7. About 550 yards; 4 feet x 1½ feet at bottom.

New trenches to be taped by 91st Field Coy. R.E.. Covering party to be found by
      7th Cameron Hrs.

                              Captain,
                              Brigade Major,
12th Septr. 1916.   44th Infantry Brigade.

To. O. C., 9th Black Watch,
       8th Seaforth Hrs.
       7th Cameron Hrs.
       9th Gordon Hrs.(Pioneers).
       91st Field Coy. R.E.
  15th Division - for information.

Operation Order No 25
— by —
Lieut Col N. A. Thomson D.S.O.
Commdg. 8th Battn Seaforth Highlrs

9th September 1916

1. The Battalion will be relieved by 4th Battn East Yorkshire Regt on night of 9th/10th Septr in the following order:—
   "B" Coy, 8th Seaforth Highlrs will be relieved by "B" Coy. 4th East Yorks, accompanied by 1 Lewis Gun per Platoon.
   "D" Coy, 8th Seaforth Highlrs will be relieved by "C" Coy. 4th East Yorks.
   "A" Coy, " "   "   "   "   "   "   "D" Coy. "   "   "
   "C" Coy, " "   "   "   "   "   "   "A" Coy. "   "   "
   Guides, (1 per Platoon) for incoming companies of 4th East Yorks, will be at N.W. Corner of MAMETZ WOOD at 2. a.m. 10th inst.
   Route for "B" & "C" Coys. East Yorks Regt. — SOMME ALLEY.

2. On relief companies of 8th Seaforth Highlrs will proceed to relieve the 24th Battn Northumberland Fusiliers as follows:—
   "B" Coy 8th Seaforth Highlrs will relieve "D" Coy. 24th Northumberland Fusiliers in the CUTTING, CONTALMAISON.
   "D" Coy 8th Seaforth Highlrs will relieve "C" Coy. 24th Northumberland Fusiliers in the CUTTING, CONTALMAISON.
   Guides (1 per Platoon) from 24th Northumberland Fusiliers for "B" & "D" Coy. will be at N.W Corner of MAMETZ WOOD at 3-45 a.m. 10th inst.
   Route:— SOMME ALLEY
   "A" Coy 8th Seaforth Highlanders will relieve "B" Coy 24th Northumberland Fus. in O.G.I. West of Railway
   "C" Coy 8th Seaforth Highlanders will relieve "A" Coy 24th Northumberland Fus. in O.G.I West of Railway.
   Guides (1 per Platoon) from 24th Northumberland Fusiliers for "A" & "C" Companies will be at S.W. Corner of BAZENTIN-LE-PETIT WOOD at 3.45 a.m. on 10th inst.
   On relief mentioned in Para 1 being complete, Battn Headquarters will move back to O.G.I.

3. All movements to be by Platoons at 400 yards interval.

4. Advanced parties of 1 Officer and 1 N.C.O. per Company from 4th Battn East Yorkshire Regt. will report at respective Company Headquarters at 6.0 pm tonight to take over Trench Stores.
   Trench stores at present in charge of 24th Northumberland Fusiliers will be taken over by Companies of 8th Seaforth Hrs on relief.
   Receipts will be taken & given, & copies forwarded to Battn Hqrs by 12 noon 10th Septr.

5. The 3 extra Lewis Guns, and teams at present attached to "B" Coy will return to Headquarters Detachment on relief.

6. No rations will be brought up tonight.
   The Transport Officer will arrange to bring rations to the CUTTING, CONTALMAISON at 6.0 a.m. tomorrow morning.

7. Completion of relief by Companies of 4th Battn East Yorks will be reported by wire or runner to Battn Hqrs.
   Companies will also report when they have taken up their new positions.

Issued through signals at 5-45 p.m.

H Blackwood Lt Captain & Adjt.
Adjt. 8th Bn Seaforth Highlrs

Distribution
Copy No 1 .... O.C. A Coy
      2 .... O.C. B Coy
      3 .... O.C. C Coy
      4 .... O.C. D Coy
      5 .... O.C. 4th Battn East Yorks Regt
      6 .... O.C. 24th Northumberland Fusiliers
      7 .... Lewis Gun Officer
      8 .... Transport Officer
      9 .... Quartermaster
     10 .... War Diary.
     11 .... File.

XXIV

Operation Order No 25
by
Lieut. Col. N. A. Thomson. DSO.
Commdg: 8th Battn Seaforth Highlrs.
12th Septr 1916.

Reference Trench Map. 57.d. S.E.

The Battn will be relieved tomorrow by the 6th Battn Cameron Highlrs as follows:-

- Companies will be relieved by corresponding Companies of 6th Cameron Highlrs.

Guides from 8th Seaforth Highlanders (1 per Platoon & 1 for Headquarters) will parade outside Battn Hqrs tomorrow at 5.45 a.m under an Officer to be detailed by O.C. "A" Coy, and march to ROUND WOOD where they will meet incoming companies at 7.0 a.m

Route for incoming Companies:- CUTTING, CONTALMAISON, PEARL ALLEY.

- On relief Companies will move back to bivouac at X.26.b.

Guides from advanced parties which proceeded today will meet them at on FRICOURT - CONTALMAISON ROAD at X.27.d.2.0.

Route:- YORKSHIRE ALLEY, THE CUTTING.

- All movements to be by Platoons at 400 yards interval.

- During the relief all troops are to keep to the trenches north of THE CUTTING.

- Companies will bring out their 50% picks & shovels.

- Trench Stores will be handed over & receipts taken; receipts to be forwarded to Battn Hqrs by 12 noon 13th Septr.

- All dixchies & mens Kit will be dumped at present cookhouse by 8.30 a.m. The Transport Officer will detail three limbers to be there at that hour.

- ~~Completion of reliefs will be reported by runner~~

- All trenches, bivouacs etc must be left scrupulously clean before handing over.

- Completion of reliefs will be reported by runner to Battn Hqrs.

- Companies will also report when they have taken up their new position.

Issued through signals at 11.30 p.m.

Copy No 1 .. O.C. "A" Coy.   No 6 .. O.C. 6th Cameron Hrs.
     2 .. O.C. "B" Coy.   7 .. Transport Officer.
     3 .. O.C. "C" Coy.   8 .. Quartermaster.
     4 .. O.C. "D" Coy.   9 .. War Diary.
     5 .. L.G.O.   10 .. File.

Hope W. Duncan Captain
Adjt. 8th Battn Seaforth Highlrs

S E C R E T.  44th Brigade.
B.M. 28

All Units, 44th Inf. Bde.

     Information has been received that previous experience shows that it is possible a counter attack in retaliation for our offensive operation to-day may be launched from the German front line in S.2.b. and S.3.a.

     Units should therefore be on the look out for any signs of hostile activity on their front and at once deal with it.

The contact aeroplane *which will fly over at 6.30 p.m. 8th inst* should be watched which will drop Smoke Bombs as an S.O.S. signal in the event of observing hostile troops massing.

Lewis Guns in advanced positions should be able to deal effectively with any hostile attack coming over the hill.

8th September 1916.

F A Beck, Major,
Brigade Major,
44th Infantry Brigade.

SECRET.   Operation Order No 24.   Copy No 6
                              by
              Lieut Col N.A. Thomson D.S.O.   XV
              Cmndg 8th Seaforth Highlanders.
Reference:- The Corps Map Sheet I.13.B. 1/10000.   8th Sept. 1916.

1. (a). On 9th September in conjunction with operations elsewhere, the
       1st Division will be attacking the Eastern portion of HIGH WOOD
       & Wood Lane.
   (b). There will be a deliberate bombardment by artillery beginning
       at 7 a.m. 9th & continuing till Zero.
   (c). Zero time will be notified later.

2. From Zero to Zero plus 15 minutes, provided the wind is favourable i.e.
   South or South-West, the 15th Division will liberate smoke along their
   whole front. This will be done by "P" bombs only from the new "jumping
   off" trench in front of CLARKS & SWANSEA TRENCHES.
   This will be done as follows:-
       (a). By 9th Black Watch for 400 yds i.e. from Head of BETHELL SAP to
           Head of Kerry Extension.
       (b). By 8th Seaforth Highrs for 300 yds from the Head of KERRY ALLEY
           Extension Westwards.
       (c). By 8/10th Gordon Highrs for 300yds from left of 8th Seaforth Highrs.
           Westwards.
   "B" Company 8th Seaforth Highrs will liberate smoke as detailed in
   Subpara (b) :- Number of bombs
                   8 for every 25 yds of front :- 8 x 12 = 96.
   Note:- 1 "P" bomb to be thrown every 2 minutes for 15 minutes.

3. In the event of wind being unfavourable code word "SCOTS" will be
   sent at Zero minus 1 hour - denoting that smoke will not be
   liberated.

4. O.C. "B" Company will detail 1 officer to be at Brigade Headquarters at
   11 a.m. on 9th inst to synchronize watches. This officer will report at Battn
   Headquarters on his return.

                                      George W. Duncan
Copy No 1. "A" Coy No 5. L.Col.O.   Captain
        2. "B" Coy No 6. Nav Diary   Adjutant 8th Battn Seaforth Highlanders
        3. "C" Coy No 7. File
        4. "D" Coy Issued at 11.20 p.m.

XXV

SECRET.   44th Brigade B.M.231.

All Units 44th Inf.Bde.

WARNING ORDER.

1. Units must be prepared to move into occupation of the following areas allotted to them on Z day. -

   "A" Battn. 8/10th Gordon Hrs.   CONTALMAISON.

       H.Qrs. CUTTING.

   "B" Battn. 8th Seaforth Hrs.   CUTTING, PEARL ALLEY and PEAKE WOOD.

       H.Qrs. PEAKE WOOD.

   "C" Battn. 9th Black Watch.   SCOTS REDOUBT.

       H.Qrs. SCOTS REDOUBT.

   "D" Battn. 7th Cameron Hrs.   SHELTER WOOD, BIRCH WOOD and ROUND WOOD.

       H.Qrs. N.E.corner of SHELTER WOOD.

   M.G.Company and T.M.Battery.   LONELY TRENCH.

2. Units should arrange to send advanced parties to their respective areas during the afternoon of the 14th Sept. *not later than 4 p.m.*

3. Brigade Headquarters will be SHELTER WOOD.

                                   Captain,
                               Brigade Major,
                        44th Infantry Brigade.

13/9/16

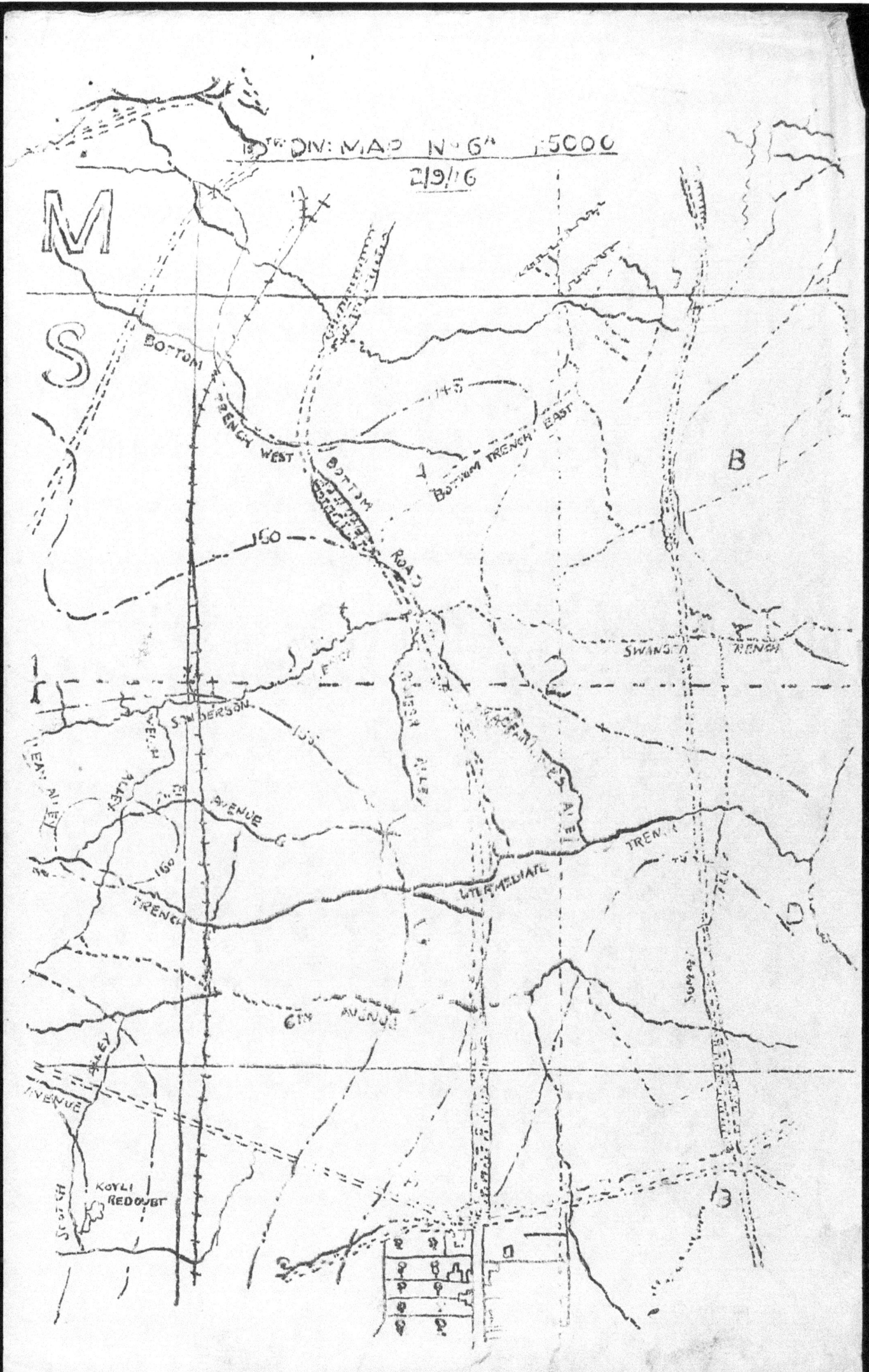

SECRET.   44th Brigade B.M.133.

All Units 44th Inf.Bde.
103rd Inf.Bde.
150th Inf.Bde.
149th Inf.Bde.
15th Division.
Staff Captain.
PROPOSED RELIEF PROGRAMME.

Night of 7/8th September.
  8th Seaforth Hrs. (in Brigade Support) to change places with 7th Cameron Hrs. and take over from 9th Black Watch that portion of CLARKS TRENCH from KERRY ALLEY to the base of BETHELL SAP (exclusive).

8th September. Reserve Battn. (8/10th Gordon Highrs.)
  44th Infantry Brigade to take over front line from Pt.S.2.b.8.4 (just west of JUTLAND ALLEY) to S.2.a.4.2.(first sap forward from SANDERSON TRENCH, West of BOTTOM ROAD inclusive) from a portion 8th Seaforth Hrs. and Right Battalion 103rd Inf.Bde.

  "A" Battn. 149th Inf.Bde. to take over QUADRANGLE from 8/10th Gordon Hrs.

  "B" Battn. 149th Inf.Bde. to take over SHELTER WOOD.

Night 9/10th September.
  "A" and "B" Battns. 149th Inf.Bde., being replaced by "A" and "B" Battalions 150th Inf.Bde., move forward and relieve Right Battalion (9th Black Watch) 44th Inf.Bde., from extreme Right of section to base of BETHELL SAP inclusive. 9th Black Watch on relief to move back to billets in ALBERT.

Night 10/11th September.
  "A" Battn. 150th Inf.Bde. relieves CENTRE Battalion (8th Seaforth Hrs.) 44th Inf.Bde., in front line from base of BETHELL SAP (exclusive) to S.2.b.8.4.
  "B" Battn. 150th Inf.Bde. relieves SUPPORT Battn.(7th Cameron Hrs.) 44th Inf.Bde., in O.G.line.
  On relief, 8th Seaforth Hrs. to relieve "Y" Battn., 103rd Inf. Bde. and 7th Cameron Hrs. to move to QUADRANGLE.

Night 10/11th September.
  44th Inf.Bde. H.Qrs. moves to SHELTER WOOD, handing over command and H.Qrs. in MAMETZ WOOD to B.G.C. 150th Inf.Bde.

11th September.
  7th Cameron Hrs. relieve 8/10th Gordon Hrs. in front line from Pt.S.2.b.8.4. to S.2.a.4.2. (The Right Section of new front of 15th Division).
  On relief 8/10th Gordons move into RESERVE Right Section.
  9th Black Watch move from ALBERT to SUPPORT Right Section.

13th September.
  45th Infantry Brigade relieves 44th Infantry Brigade in Right Section.
  On relief 44th Infantry Brigade moves into Divisional Reserve area East and S.W. of ALBERT.

  Note. Vickers Guns and Stokes Mortars to be xxxxxxxxxxxxxx relieved with the Sub-sections to which they are attached.

6-9-16.

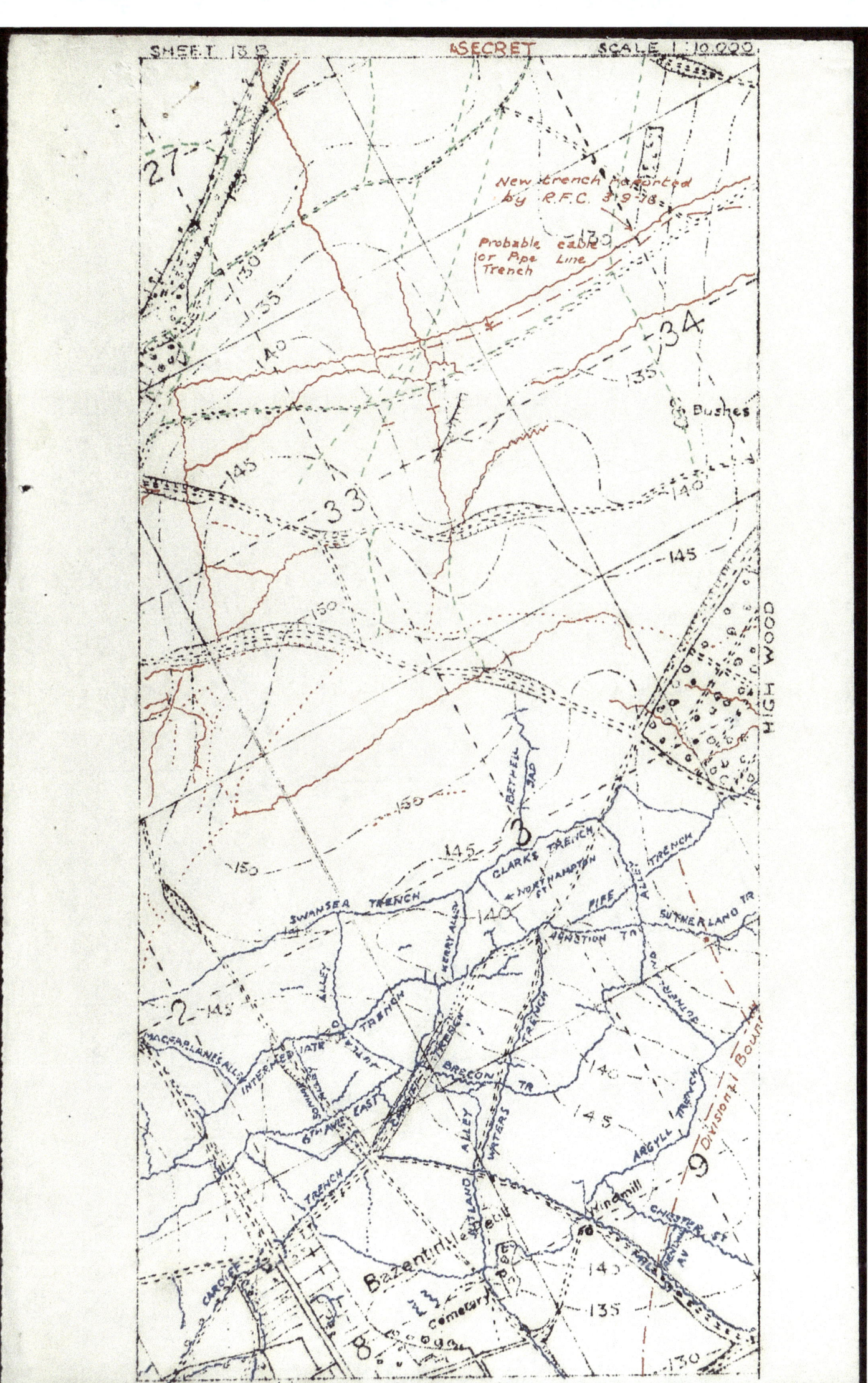

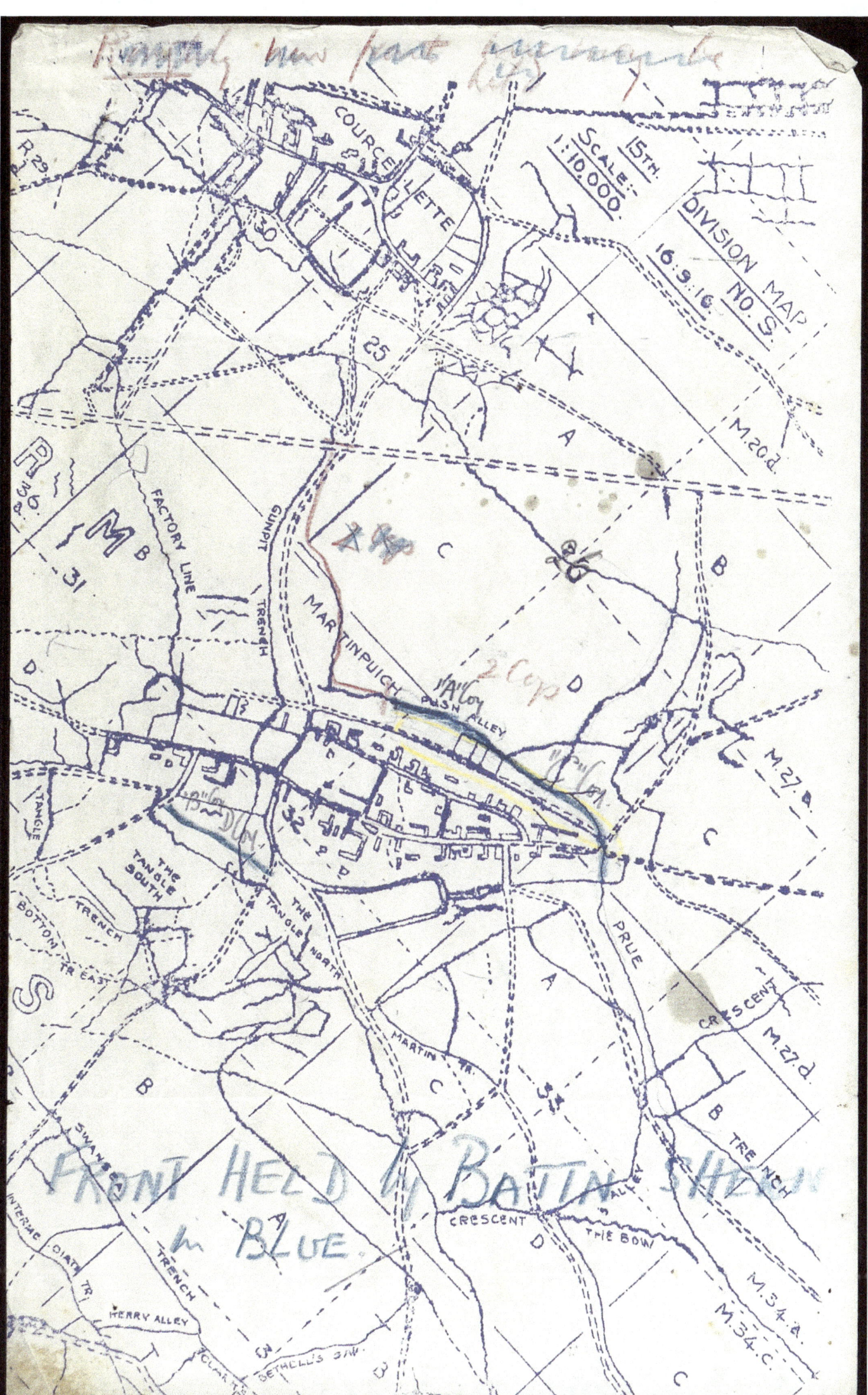

SECRET

Operation Order No. 27.
by
Lieut. Col. C. A. Thomson D.S.O.
Commanding 8th Battn. Seaforth Highlanders

Copy No. 8

14th September 1916.

1. The Battalion will move into a forward reserve area tonight as follows :—

   "A" & "C" Companies to THE CUTTING, CONTALMAISON.
   "B" & "D" Companies to PEARL ALLEY and PEAKE WOOD.
   Headquarters to PEAKE WOOD.
   Order of March :— "A" "C" "B" "D" Companies
   The 1st Platoon of "A" Coy to move at 7-15 p.m.
   Route — ALBERT – BECOURT – LOZENGE WOOD ROAD.
   All movements to be by platoons at 200 yards interval.
   N.C.O's who proceeded today with advance party will meet their respective Companies on main FRICOURT – CONTALMAISON ROAD and guide them to their positions.

2. All packs, greatcoats & Officers Valises will be stacked by Companies by 7 p.m.
   The Transport Officer will arrange to send these to Quartermasters Stores.

3. ½ a limber per Coy and one for Headquarters will be at camp at 7-15 p.m. to transport kitchens and Officers Mess Kit to new positions.

4. Companies will report by runner to Battn. Hqrs when they have taken up their new positions.

George W Duncan
Caplin
Adjutant : 8th Battn Seaforth Highlanders

Distribution :—

Copy No 1	O.C. "A" Coy	Copy No 6	Transport Officer
2	O.C. "B" Coy	7	Quartermaster
3	O.C. "C" Coy	8	War Diary
4	O.C. "D" Coy	9	File
5	L.G.O.		

Issued at 5.45 p.m.

15th DIVISION SUMMARY of OPERATIONS.

6 A.M. 15-9-16 to 7-30 A.M. 16-9-16.

OPERATIONS.

At 6-20 A.M. (15-9-16) our troops launched their assault on enemy trenches South and South-west of MARTINPUICH from the new jumping-off trenches dug in the course of the last week in front of SANDERSON and CAMERON TRENCHES. There was no preliminary intense bombardment but the hostile positions had been subjected to a steady and continuous shelling from guns of all calibres for several days beforehand. During the previous night Battalions moved into position for the assault, the boundaries between the assaulting Brigades being the Road running North and South in S.1.b. At Zero the infantry left their trenches and an intense barrage was opened on the German trenches and also a creeping barrage which lifted 50 yards a minute. The final objective was to be reached by the Right Brigade in one bound, except for a short length of its left which was thrown back to link up with the Right of the Left Brigade, who were obtaining their final objective in two bounds. The first objectives were taken without difficulty, the enemy showing little inclination to fight and being taken completely by surprise. Many prisoners were taken especially by the Left Brigade. At twentyfive minutes after Zero the assault on the final objective started, the extreme left being a point in the FACTORY LINE about 250 yards from the Railway at M.32.a.2.0., thence along the trench, through the outskirts of the Village to join up with the Right Brigade. More prisoners were taken and both Brigades started to consolidate the positions won, these consisting of FACTORY LINE, TANGLE TRENCH, THE TANGLE SOUTH and BOTTOM TRENCH EAST and WEST. At 3 hours after Zero our heavy artillery lifted beyond MARTINPUICH and strong patrols were sent out into the Village. These found the N.E. end to be occupied and they were received with machine gun fire. But they succeeded in bringing back several more prisoners from dug-outs including a battalion Commander and his adjutant. The patrols up the S.W. end of the Village found it empty. Meantime the Division on our Right had gained its third objective and had captured PRUE TRENCH, and in order to link up with them at the N.E. end of the Village both our Brigades attacked at 3 P.M. The Left Brigade met with no opposition and occupied the portion of PUSH ALLEY allotted to them, and also the end of GUNPIT TRENCH. The Right Brigade swept through the N.E. portion of the Village and, after some bombing, forced all the garrison to surrender, capturing in this part alone nearly 200 prisoners. A line was then established in continuation of PUSH ALLEY parallel to and N. of the Railway up to the Cross Roads at M.27.c.2.1. where connection should have been made with the Division on our Right. Unfortunately whilst our troops were undertaking this operation theirs were shelled out of PRUE TRENCH. During the night a trench was dug connecting our line North of MARTINPUICH with PRUE TRENCH, a Post being established in the latter which appeared to be quite unoccupied. The whole of the captured positions were then consolidated. Wiring was carried out with materials from a captured German dump. In the afternoon work was started on communication trenches and this was continued during the night. GORDON ALLEY was carried right through to FACTORY LINE and GUNPIT TRENCH, and WELCH ALLEY to TANGLE TRENCH and the TANGLE SOUTH. The attack was assisted by a Tank. This machine did not cross our front line until after the infantry had started owing to the exceptionally difficult nature of the ground but it eventually reached the S.W. end of MARTINPUICH where it halted. About mid-day it returned to re-fit and in the evening made another trip to the S.W. end of MARTINPUICH where it deposited some ammunition and returned to re-fit again. The exact number of prisoners taken is not clear because practically all from the Left Brigade failed to pass through the Divisional collecting Station at MIDDLE WOOD and many others were diverted to various fatigue duties, such as stretcher bearers, before reaching MIDDLE WOOD. The captured however, number between 600 and 700 and belonged to the following Regiments:- 133rd Reserve, 211th Res.

P.T.O.

17th, 18th and 23rd Bavarian, 19th Foot Artillery, 40th Reserve Field Artillery Regt and 167th Machine Gun Company.   At present 3 machine guns and 1 gun in MARTINPUICH have been reported captured.   Further details will be given later when known.

PRESENT FRONT LINE.

On the right the line last night ran from T.21.B in the centre of BOULEUX WOOD to T.15.central, thence to T.9.d.7.8., through T.3.central to N.32.d.9.1., round the Northern edge of FLERS to M.36.a., thence due West to Northern edge of MARTINPUICH, N.W. round COURCELETTE the whole of which has been captured, to M.28.c.9.6., and thence South of MOUQUET FARM on the original line.   Our Corps took 37 Officers and 1,300 other ranks, Centre Corps 7 Officers and 262 other ranks, Right Corps 30 Officers and 289 other ranks.   The Corps on our left took over 600 prisoners.

During the day on the British front 12 hostile aeroplanes were driven down, crashing to the earth, and 7 others were forced to descend, apparently out of control.   In addition two kite balloons were destroyed during the day.

FRENCH COMMUNIQUE.   AFTERNOON 16-9-16.

North of the SOMME the French attacked South of RANCOURT and reached the edge of the Village.   North of FARM LE PRIEZ we advanced 500 metres and the surrounding of COMBLES is in good progress.   We are pushing North of BOUCHAVESNES – East of route de BETHUNE – East of DENIECOURT and North-east of BERNY.   200 prisoners including 5 officers were taken and 10 machine guns.   The enemy's casualties were very heavy.

SALONICA.   MAKUKOVO has been captured by the British.   100 prisoners were taken and 10 machine guns.   On the Right bank of the River VARDAR the French advanced on a front of 1,500 metres with a depth of 800 metres. East of River TOERVA the Servians are steadily advancing.   West of MONT OSTROVO the heavy fighting between the Servian Troops and very important Bulgarian forces is turning to the advantage of the Servians.   They have just had a brilliant success as a result of which GORNICEVO and the heights of MALKANIDZE are in their hands.   Servian Cavalry is chasing the routed enemy and have taken the Village of EKSISU – 25 guns and many prisoners (number not yet known) have been captured.

ROUMANIAN FRONT.   The Roumanians are steadily advancing in TRANSYLVANIA BAROT and ITHBAGAT have been captured.   (BAROT is situated in TRANSYLVANIA, 50 miles from the ROUMANIAN Frontier.

C.N.RYAN, Captain, G.S.
for Lieut Colonel,
General Staff, 15th Division.

S E C R E T.   Copy No. 2

44th Infantry Brigade Operation Order No.92.
_____

12-9-16.

Reference Map.
ALBERT Combined Sheet 1/10,000.

1. The 45th Infantry Brigade will relieve the 44th Infantry Brigade in the Right Section, Left Sector, III Corps, on the 13th September, in accordance with table on reverse.

2. All movements to be by platoons at not less than 100 yards interval.

3. During the relief all troops are to keep in the trenches East of O.G.line.

4. All trench stores will be collected at convenient places and handed over. Receipts to be sent to the Brigade Office by 10 A.M. 14th instant.

   Units will bring out their 50% picks and shovels.

5. Three mortars, of mortars in the line, to be handed over to the teams of the 45th T.M.Battery.

6. The Nos.1 of each machine gun and each mortar will remain in line until their services can be dispensed with.

7. Battalions 1st Line Transport, with the exception of water carts and cookers, remain in their present position.

8. Units will send advanced parties on the evening of the 12th to the units they will relieve.

9. Completion of reliefs will be reported by wire to Brigade Headquarters which, on completion of relief, will re-open at Pt.W.29.d.3.3.

10. Acknowledge.

Issued through
   Signals.
   3-30 P.M.

Captain,
Brigade Major,
44th Infantry Brigade.

Copies to :-
   No. 1. 9th Black Watch.
       2. 8th Seaforth Hrs.
       3. 8/10th Gordons.
       4. 7th Camerons.
       5. 44th M.G.Coy.
       6. 44th T.M.Battery.
       7. 15th Div.
       8. 45th Inf.Bde.
       9. 46th Inf.Bde.
      10. 149th Inf.Bde.
      11. 150th Inf.Bde.
      12. 91st Fld.Coy.R.E.
      13. Bde.Transport Officer.
      14. Bde. Supply Offcr.
      15. No.2 Coy.Train.
      16. Bde.Signal Offcr.
      17. 17th Div.Arty.
      18. 15th Div.Arty.
      19. III Corps H.A.
      20. 45th Fld.Amb.
      21. Staff Capt.
      22. War Diary.
      23. File.
      24. Spare.

Table to accompany 45th Infantry Brigade Operation Order No.92, dated 12-9-16.

Unit of 45th Inf.Bde.	Unit of 44th Inf.Bde. to be relieved.	STARTING POINT. Place.	Guides.	Time. A.M.	Route for Units relieving.	Destination of Unit being relieved, and Unit from which it will take over.
6/7th R.S.Fus:	"A" Battn. 7th Cameron Hrs.	Junction CUTTING and PEARL ALLEY.	1 per platoon. 1 Battn.H.Q.	5-0	WELCH ALLEY.	Bivouac at Pt.E.7. Central. 11th A.& S.Hrs.
45th M.G.Coy.	41th M.G.Coy.	- do -	1 per gun for guns in line.	6-0	Most convenient.	45th M.G.Coy. - do -
45th T.M.Bty.	44th T.M.Btty.	- do -	- do -	6-30	- do -	Bivouac at Pt.E.5.b. 45th T.M.Bty.
6th Cam.Hrs.	"B" Battn. 8th Seaforth Hrs.	ROUND WOOD.	1 per platoon. 1 Battn.H.Q.	7-0	- do -	Bivouac at Pt.X.28.b. 5/7th R.S.Fusrs:
11th A.& S.H.	"C" Battn. 8/10th Gordons.	Junction LOZENGE WOOD with FRICOURT	- do -	8-0	- do -	Bivouac at Pt.W.29.d. 6th Cameron Hrs.
13th R.Scots.	"D" Battn. 9th Black Watch.	CONTALMAISON Road.	- do -	9-0	- do -	Bivouac at Pt.E.7. Central. 13th Royal Scots.

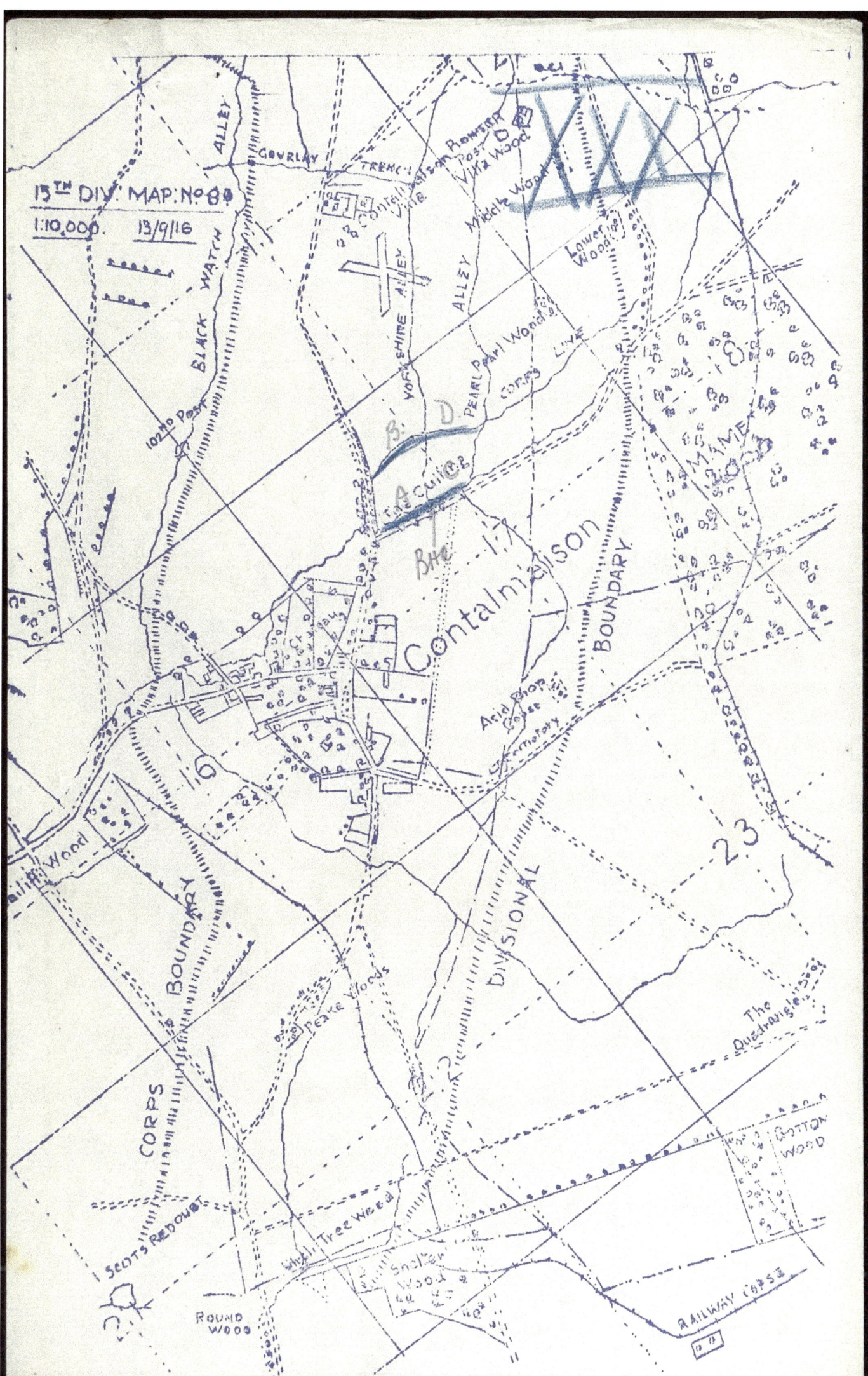

SECRET.   Copy No. 2

44th Infantry Brigade Operation Order No.93.

14-9-16.

Reference Maps.
  ALBERT Combined Sheet 1/10,000.
  and 57.D.4. 1/10,000.

1. In accordance with 15th Division Operation Order No.90 of the 12th September, the 44th Infantry Brigade will move into a forward Divisional Reserve Area on 14th Sept.

2. Units will move to the following destinations :-

    9th Black Watch.   SCOTS REDOUBT.
          H.Qrs. SCOTS REDOUBT.
        Starting Point ARBRE TREFLE on ALBERT-BECOURT Road.
        Time 8 P.M.

    8th Seaforth Hrs.   CUTTING, PEARL ALLEY and PEAKE WOOD.
          H.Qrs. PEAKE WOOD.
        Start from Camp 7-15 P.M.

    8/10th Gordon Hrs. CONTALMAISON.
          H.Qrs. CONTALMAISON.
        Starting Point ARBRE TREFLE on ALBERT - BECOURT Road.
        Time 7-15 P.M.

    7th Cameron Hrs.   SHELTER WOOD, BIRCH WOOD and ROUND WOOD.
          H.Qrs. N.E.corner of SHELTER WOOD.
        Start from Camp at 7-45 P.M.

    44th M.G.Company.   LONELY TRENCH.
        To start when 7th Cameron Hrs. are clear.

    44th T.M.Battery.   LONELY TRENCH.
        To start when 9th Black Watch are clear.

3. Units will move via the ALBERT - BECOURT - LOZENGE WOOD Road by platoons at 200 yards interval E.of ALBERT.

4. Brigade Headquarters will close at W.29.d.3.8. at 9 P.M. and open simultaneously at SHELTER WOOD.

5. With reference to operations :-
        A Battalion will be the 8/10th Gordon Hrs.
        B   "   "   "   " 8th Seaforth Hrs.
        C   "   "   "   " 9th Black Watch.
        D   "   "   "   " 7th Cameron Hrs.

Issued Through   Captain,
  Signals.   Brigade Major,
  2-30 P.M.   44th Infantry Brigade.

Copies to :-
    No. 1. 9th Black Watch.   No.13. Bde.Transport Offcr.
        2. 8th Seaforth Hrs.   14. Bde. Supply Offcr.
        3. 8/10th Gordon Hrs.   15. Bde.Signal Offcr.
        4. 7th Cameron Hrs.   16. Bde.Bombing Offcr.
        5. 44 M.G.Coy.   17. No.2 Coy.Train.
        6. 44th T.M.Battery.   18. 15th Div.Arty.
        7. 15th Div.   19. 47th Div.Arty.
        8. 45th Inf.Bde.   20. III Corps H.A.
        9. 46th Inf.Bde.   21. 45th Fld.Amb.
       10. 149th Inf.Bde.   22. Staff Captain.
       11.   Canadian Div.   23. War Diary.
       12. 91st Fld.Coy.R.E.   24. File.

44th Brigade B.M.197.

8th Seaforths.
8/10th Gordons.
7th Camerons.
74th Fld.Coy.R.E.

1. The following trenches will be completed to a depth of four feet, and waved.

2. On the night 10/11th September the 8/10th Gordon Hrs. will dig a trench marked A in sketch from S.1.d.6½.9. to the road at S.1.d.3.9½. Total length to be dug about 200 yards.

3. On the night of the 10/11th September the 7th Cameron Hrs. will dig a trench marked B in sketch from S.1.b.9½.1. to the road at S.1.b.5.3. Total length about 300 yards.

4. On the night of 11/12th September the 8th Seaforth Hrs. will dig a trench from S.2.a.4.3. to the road at S.1.b.7.6½. marked C in sketch. Total length about 450 yards.

5. The 74th Fld.Coy.R.E. will tape out the sites and have them ready for work to be commenced at dark each of the two nights mentioned.

6. On the night of 10/11th September the 8/10th Gordon Hrs. will find the covering party for both parties digging.
   On the night of 11/12th the 7th Cameron Hrs. will find the covering party.

7. The digging of these trenches will take precedence of all other work. The G.O.C. wishes to impress upon the battalion commanders concerned that it is of the utmost importance that their tasks should be completed on nights allotted to them.

8. These trenches will be continued West of the road by the 103rd Brigade.

Captain,
Brigade Major,
44th Infantry Brigade.

10-9-16.

SECRET

Operation Order No. 29.
— by —
Lieut. Col. M. A. Thomson D.S.O.
Commdg. 8th Battn Seaforth Highlanders

XXXII
Copy No. 9

17th Septr 1916

Reference 15th Div Map No. 8ᴬ dated 13-9-16.
              "   "   No. 5.   "   16-9-16.

1. The Battalion will move today to take over the front line now held by the 45th Infty Bde as follows :—

(a) "A" & "C" Companies will take over front line now held by 6/7th Royal Scots Fusiliers from Pt. M.32.a.9.9. to M.27.c.2.1. with "A" Coy on the left and "C" Coy on the right.
    The Dividing line between the two Companies to be decided and reported to Battn Hqrs by O.C. "A" Coy on relief.

(b) "B" & "D" Companies will move into support in positions now occupied by 11th Argyll & Sutherland Highrs.

(c) Battn Headquarters will move to K.O.Y.L.I. TRENCH near K.O.Y.L.I. REDOUBT.

2. Companies will move in following order :— "D", "B", "A" & "C" Coys.
   Guides (1 per platoon) (for "D" & "B" Coys) will be at junction of WELCH ALLEY and SANDERSON TRENCH at 6-0 p.m.
   Guides (1 per platoon) for "A" & "C" Companies will be at above rendezvous at 7 p.m.
   All movements to be by platoons at 400 yds interval.

3. Completion of reliefs to be reported by runner to Battn Hqrs.
   All Trench stores will be taken over by Companies on relief. Lists of stores taken over will be forwarded to Battn Hqrs as soon as possible.

4. Tomorrows rations will be carried on the man.
   As much water as possible will be carried up by companies.

Issued through signals at 4-15. p.m.

George W. Duncan
Captain
Adjt. 8th Battn Seaforth Highlanders

Distribution.
Copy No. 1. O.C. "A" Coy.
        2. O.C. "B" Coy.
        3. O.C. "C" Coy.
        4. O.C. "D" Coy.
        5. L.G.O.
        6. O.C. 11th Argyll & Sutherland Highrs.
        7. O.C. 6/7 Royal Scots Fusiliers
        8. Transport Officer.
        9. War Diary.
       10. File.

SECRET

Operation Order No 32.
by
Lieut. Col. R. A. Thomson D.S.O.
Commdg: 8th Battn Seaforth Highlanders
XXXIX
19th Sept. 1916

Reference Map, AMIENS Sheet 1/100000.

1. The Battalion will march tomorrow to FRANVILLERS as follows:—

    Starting Point :— Cross Roads, 200 yards S.W. of Church LAVIÉVILLE

    Time :— 9-55 a.m.

    Order of March :— "B", "C" "D" "A" Coys

    Route :— Main ALBERT – AMIENS ROAD.

2. Billeting Party, 1 N.C.O. per Coy, and 1 for Headqrs on bycycles will parade outside Battn Headqrs at 6-30 a.m. under 2/Lieut. J. M. Ross.

3. 1st Line Transport will march in rear of the Battn.

Mess Boxes will be collected at 9-30 a.m.

Officers valises will be taken to Quartermasters Stores by 9-15 a.m. on 20th inst.

4. 2/Lieut. G. G. Blackwood will march in rear of 1st Line Transport. All details other than drivers & brakesmen will march under this officer.

The Transport Officer will send any men who fall out on the march to report to him.

Not more than two cooks will march with each cooker.

        George W. Duncan
        ————————— Captain
        Adjt: 8th Battn Seaforth Highlanders

Issued through signals at .... a.m.

Distribution

Copy No 1 – O.C. "A" Coy   Copy No 6 – Transport Officer
        2 – O.C. "B" Coy   7 – Quartermaster
        3 – O.C. "C" Coy   8 – War Diary
        4 – O.C. "D" Coy   9 – File
        5 – L.G.O.

SECRET. 44th Brigade B.M.109.

All Units 44th Inf. Bde.

WARNING ORDER.

Reference relief of 46th Infantry Brigade on 5th instant, the following arrangements will probably hold good.

(a) The 2 left companies of the Left Front Battalion will relieve early (5-30 A.M.) they will be followed, after an interval, by the two remaining companies.
After an interval the two rear companies of the Right Front Battalion will relieve.
The Support Battalion will then relieve, then the Reserve Battalion, and finally - in the evening at dusk - the two front companies of the Right Front Battalion.

(b) Trench Mortars (of which two are in the line and two in reserve at Brigade H.Q.) will relieve about 5 A.M. on the 5th.

(c) Vickers guns (of which there are 6 in the line) will relieve on the early morning of the 5th at the same time as Trench Mortars.

2. The following will be the disposition of the Brigade :-

    Right Front Battalion.   9th Black Watch.
    Left Front Battalion.   7th Cameron Hrs.
    Support Battalion.   8th Seaforth Hrs.
    Reserve Battalion.   8/10th Gordon Hrs.

3. Officers to reconnoitre Right and Left Front Battalion trenches will go to Brigade Headquarters, 46th Inf.Bde., MAMETZ WOOD, Pt.X.24.a.9.8. at 6 A.M. to-morrow, 4th, where guides to respective Battn. H.Q. will be provided.
Officers of Support Battalion to reconnoitre accommodation will go to Battalion Headquarters in O.G.1. Pt.S.13.b.2.9.
Headquarters of Reserve Battalion (10th Sco:Rifles) are in QUADRANGLE.

4. O.C.44th M.G.Company and 44th T.M.Battery will get into touch with their opposite numbers in 46th Infantry Brigade to-morrow morning (4th) to arrange details of the relief.

5. In reconnoitring the front line positions Officers Commanding Battalions will bear in mind the strength of their battalions and ensure that they do not replace a company 100 strong xxxx by a company 150 strong. Accommodation for the extra men should be found in depth so as not to over-crowd the front system.

                                          Major,
                                   Brigade Major,
                                44th Infantry Brigade.

3-9-16.

ISSUED WITH 15TH DIVISION LETTER NO. 108/1.G. 5.9.16.

Work Report to 6 a.m. 8th Sept 1916

VIII

1. Swansea Trench & CLARKE'S TRENCH were deepened & firesteps put in -
From S.2.b.4.2 to about S.2.b.8.2 the trench is now about 5ft 6ins deep from S.2.b.8.2 to S.3.c.3.9 it is about 3ft deep on the average. From S.3.c.3.9 to S.3.c.9.9 the depth is about 5ft 6ins - work is being continued on the shallow parts.

2. Kerry Alley Extension was worked on -
This trench is now an average depth of 3ft 6ins for about 150 yds.
This sap is about 180 yds from our present front line to a pt at the head where the RE were working on the T head.

3. Party worked from the future end of SUTLAND SAP extension, eastwards for about 120 yds making a trench, along that length of front, 4ft by 5ft.

4. New trench from S.2.b.3.2½ to S.2.d.8.8. was deepened & firestepped & extended eastward for a short distance (about 20 yds)

George W Duncan
for O. S/Brattingham Capt & Adj

8/9/16.

Copy

Intelligence Report to 8am 8/9/16.

XII

1. Two enemy aeroplanes flew over our line where JUTLAND ALLEY cut SWANSEA TRENCH at 6.20am this morning.
They were only 3 or 400 ft from the ground & were fired at by our Lewis Guns & rifles. They retired immediately under cover of the mist to their own lines.

2. New trench from pt S.2.d.5.8½ to pt S.2.d.88 was intermittently shelled during the night with light guns from a north easterly direction.

3. KERRY & JUTLAND Extensions were shelled during the night while work was being carried out on them with light guns from a north easterly direction. Swansea Trench was also shelled.

4. No patrols went out as work was in progress which was covered by a party of 1 officer & 20 men.

8/9/16.

Jn Cunnnzy
Lieut Col.
Cmdg 8th Seaforth Highrs.

Work Report to 6am 9/9/16

XIII

1. New "jumping off" trench between KERRY Extension & JUTLAND Extension was worked on & is now on an average 4ft deep.
Jutland Extension itself is not yet complete & in places KERRY ALLEY still requires deepening.
It is however now possible to get right round the loop altho' in some parts of the two extensions one has to crawl.

2. SWANSEA TRENCH & CLARKS TRENCH were worked upon & are now an average depth of 5ft between JUTLAND ALLEY & NORTHAMPTON Street, 4 new firesteps were made in Swansea Trench.
Working on this trench was greatly hindered by the constant passage of troops & evacuation of wounded, Jutland Alley being used as a communication trench (up & down) not only by companies but by Pioneers & 4th Black Watch in addition.

2RE etc

9/9/16.   Cmdg 8/Sea H'rs Lt Col.

Intelligence Summary XIV 9 a.m. 9th Sept 1916

1. During the last 24 hours the Battalion frontage has been continuously shelled with L.A. & guns but no heavier guns have been used.
A great deal of this shelling came from the direction of FLERS.

2. At 6pm enemy were seen to put up red light which broke into 2 parts, from High Wood. The same lights were put up at about 11pm opposite this Battn front & immediately afterwards no mans land was heavily barraged by enemy guns.
It is thought that our parties covering our work may have been seen by the enemy & has made the enemy believe that we were attacking.
During the night the enemy appeared to be very nervous in our immediate front.

3. During yesterday morning (8th inst) several small parties of the enemy were seen moving about HIGH WOOD at S.4.a - These parties came under the fire of our field artillery.

4. During the night there was some hostile sniping & machine gun fire. The increase in enemy's machine gun activity has been be. marked in this direction.
The source was difficult to locate but a good deal

At long range behind
the fire appears to have come upon
the knoll in S.3.a & S.3.b.

9/9/16.

[signature] Lt Colonel
Cmndg 8th Seaforth Highlanders.

SECRET. 44th Bde BM 102.

All Units 44th Inf Bde.

1. The 1st Division will, on 3rd September, in conjunction with operations elsewhere, attack the German front line from S.10.b.9½.8. to where it strikes the western edge of HIGH WOOD about S.3.d.9.8
 Zero time for this attack will be intimated later.

2. There will be a deliberate bombardment by the Heavy Artillery commencing at 8 A.M. on the 2nd Sept and continuing until Zero on 3rd.

3. On Sept 2nd from 2 P.M. to 2-20 P.M. and on Sept 3rd from 5 A.M. to 5-20 A.M. the 15th Div, provided the wind is favourable, will liberate smoke along their whole front.

Labeck. Major
Bde Major
44th Inf Bde

1/9/16.

SECRET

44th Brigade.
B.M. 102.

All Units 44th Inf. Bde.

      Reference this office B.M. 102 dated 1/9/16, Zero hour will be

        12 NOON September 3rd.

2nd September 1916.

                      Major,
                Brigade Major,
            44th Infantry Brigade.

SECRET.   44th I.B. BM.177
                    8.9.16.

CORRECTION No.2/1 to 44th Inf. Bde. O.O. No 89.

Ref para. 2 – 1st line
"From zero plus 15 minutes."
should read –
From zero, to zero plus 15 minutes.

Copies to –   E A Beck. Bde Major.
1. 6th Blackwatch.   44th Inf. Bde.
2. 7th Seaforths.
3. 8/10th Gordons.
4. 7th Camerons.
5. 15th Division.
6. 2nd Inf. Bde.
7. 108th Inf. Bde.

8th Seaforth Hdrs.   SECRET 44 I.B.
                                              BM 174
Correction No. 1. to 44 I.B. OO No. 89.

Cancel para. 2. b and

Substitute :-

   8th Seaforth Highrs for 300 yards
of front - Left of 9th Black Watch
Westwards
number of bombs
     8 for every 25 yards of front
  8 × 12 = 96

   8/10 Gordons for 300 yards
of front - Left of 8th Seaforth H.
Westwards
number of bombs
     8 for every 25 yards of front
  8 × 12 = 96

                                      EaBeck. Major
8/9/16   Brig Major 44 I.B.

S E C R E T.   44th Brigade B.M.153-

All Units 44th Inf.Bde.
   74th Fld.Coy.R.E.

1. It is important that there should be no further delay in the work, forward of CLARKS and SANDERSON TRENCHES. The completion of the forward saps from these two trenches - the joining of the heads of the saps to form a new line must be pushed forward with all speed.

   All other work must give way to it and it must be completed throughout to a depth of at least 4 feet before the Brigade hands over to the 50th Division at noon on the 10th instant.

2. The Brigade Commander wishes it to be understood that this is an important operation and anything short of concentrated hostile fire must not be taken as a reason for discontinuing work.

7-9-16.

                             Major,
                         Brigade Major,
                     44th Infantry Brigade.

SECRET

Correction No 1 to Operation Order No 25 d/ 9/9/16.

XVII

1. Reference para 1:-
"A" & "C" Coys will not be relieved by companies of 4th East Yorks as detailed therein – guides will not therefore be sent by "A" & "C" Companies 8th Sea Hrs.

2. Reference para 2:-
"B" Company 8th Sea Highrs will relieve "B" Coy 24th Northd Fus in O.G.1 west of railway.
"D" Company 8th Sea Highrs will relieve "C" Coy 24th Northd Fus in O.G.1 west of railway.
Guides for these two Companies from 24th Northd Fus will be at S.W. corner of BAZENTIN-LE-PETIT WOOD at 3.45 a.m.
"C" Company 8th Sea Highrs will move to O.G.2 at 6 a.m. tomorrow.
"A" Company 8th Sea Highrs will move to O.G.2 at 6.20 a.m. tomorrow.
O.C. "A" & "C" Companies will arrange to reconnoitre O.G.2 at dawn tomorrow.

George W. Duncan.
Captain
8th Battn Seaforth Highlanders.

9/9/16.
To
All recipients of Operation Order No 25 d/9/9/16.

ISSUED THROUGH SIGNALS 11 p.m.

XIX

Intelligence Report to 7.30 am 10th Sept 1916.

1. My battalion frontage was intermittently shelled with light guns during the past 24 hours. This shelling appeared to come from the direction of MARTINPUICH in a north-easterly direction. At about midnight, about 10 4.2's were fired on junction of KERRY ALLEY & CLARKE'S TRENCH from north easterly direction.

2. Enemy machine gun previously located at S.3.b.1.8 was active during the night. Hostile sniping continued during the night.

3. Observing from M S.2.b.9½.4 our men could be seen in enemy's trenches in S.2.b.

4. No signs of new enemy work was observed.

5. Between 2pm & 3pm several shells from our field guns dropped immediately behind our "jumping off" trench about pt S.3.c.0.4.

6. At 5.35 pm one of our aeroplanes was observed to fall in flames west of BAZENTIN-LE-PETIT WOOD — exact location unknown.

Lt Colonel
Comdg 8/Sco Rifles

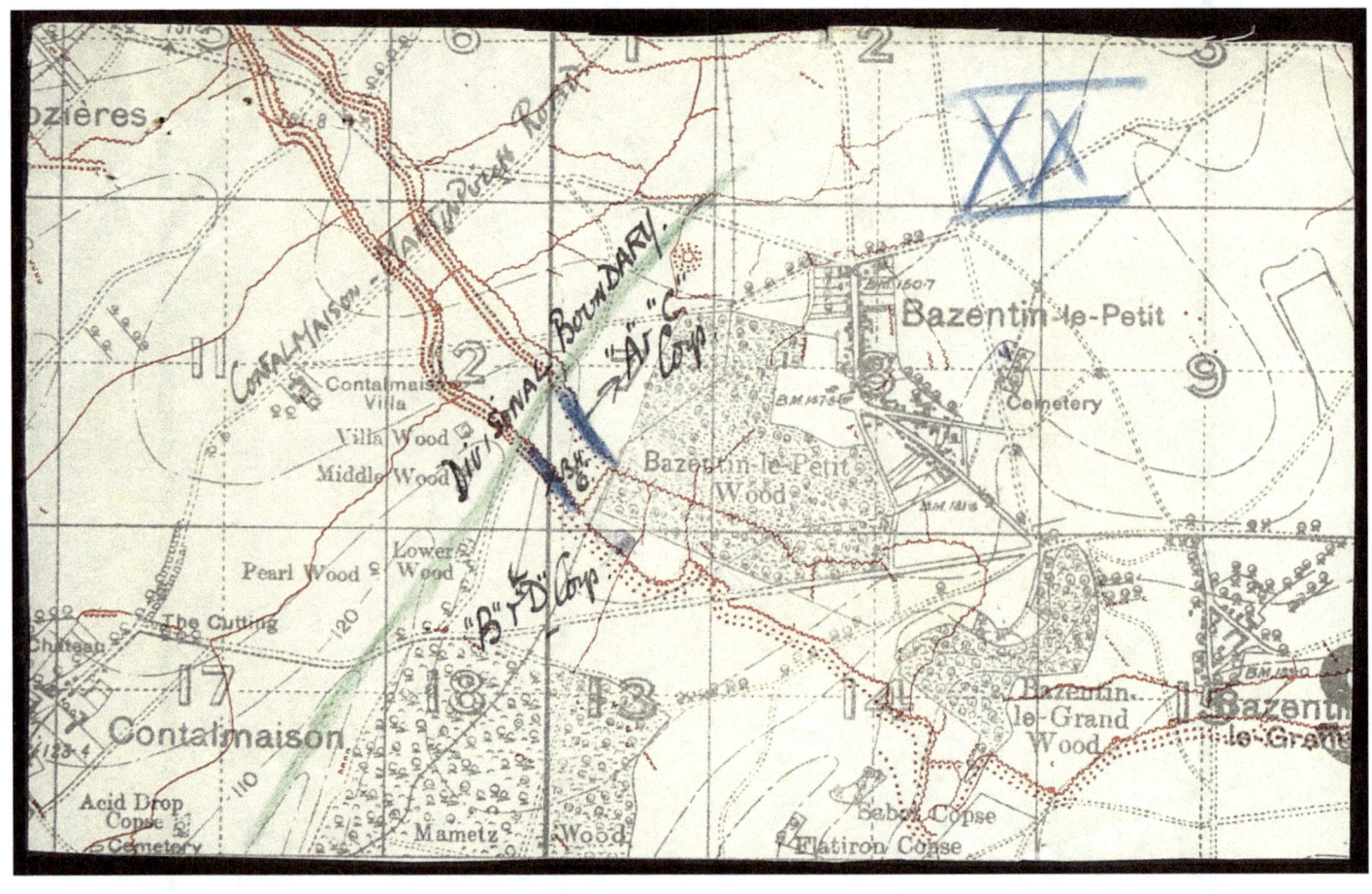

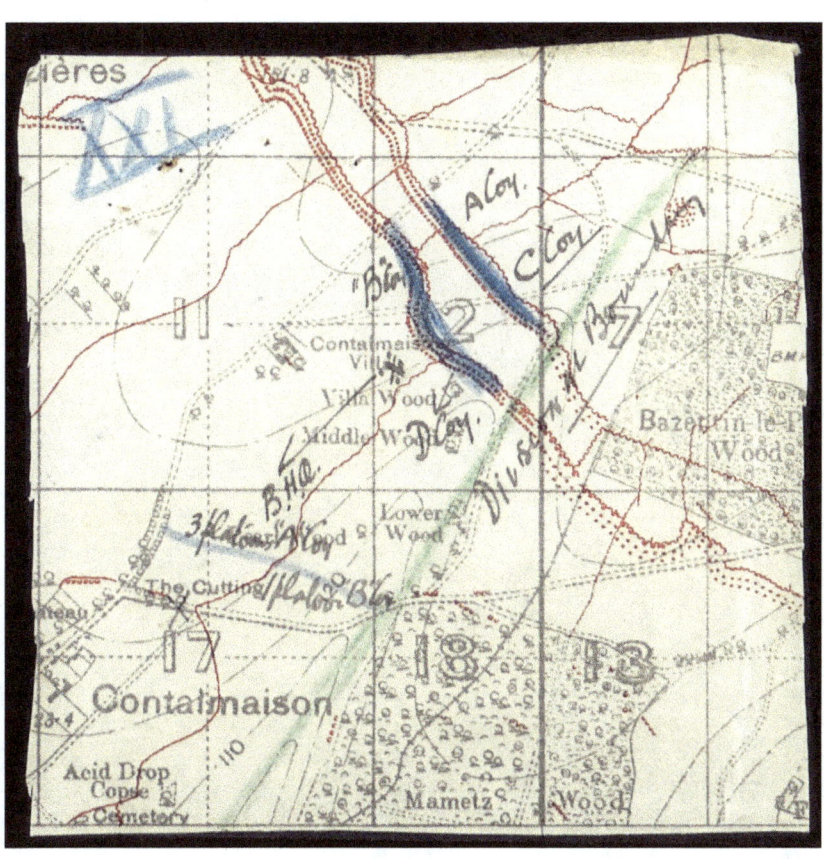

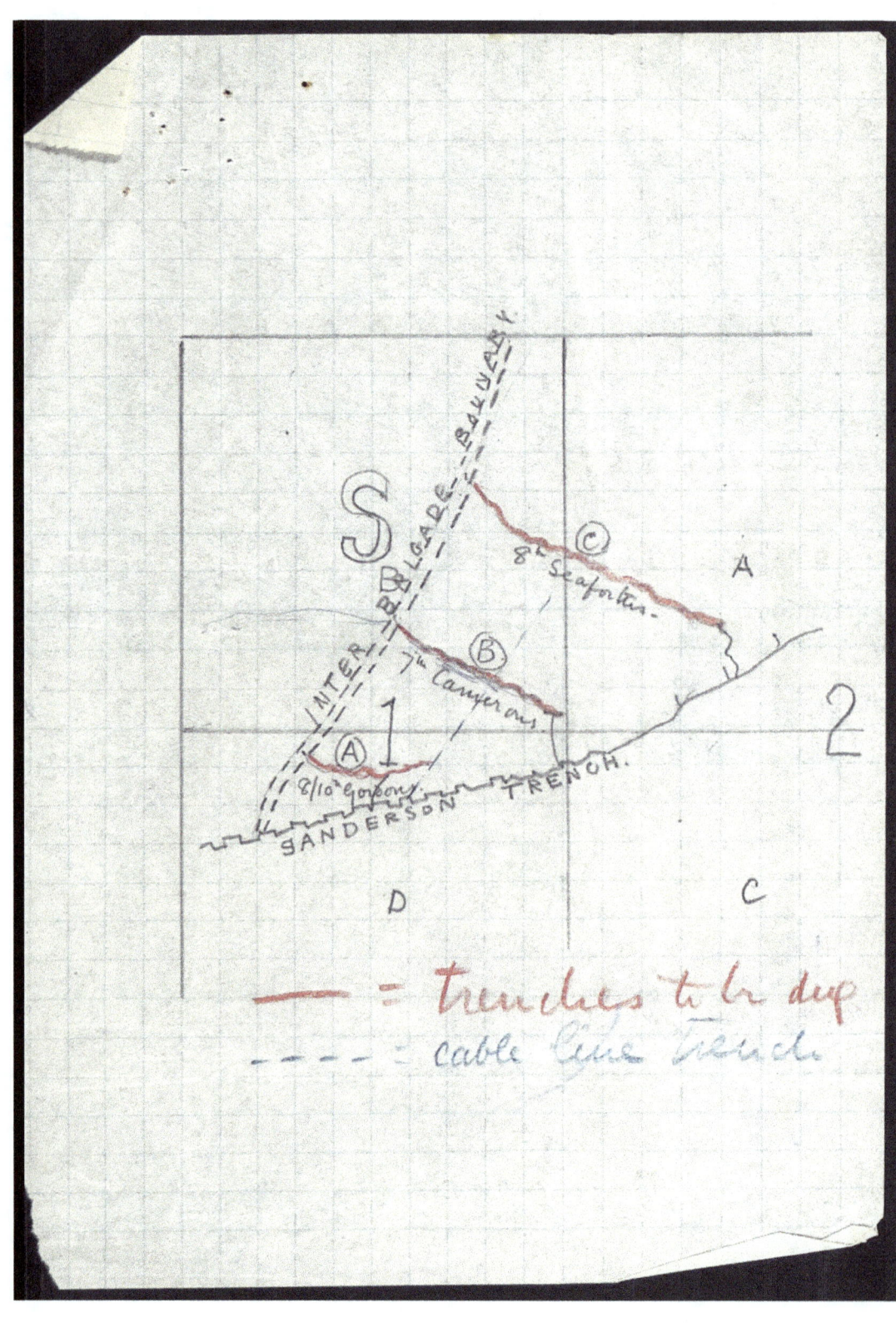

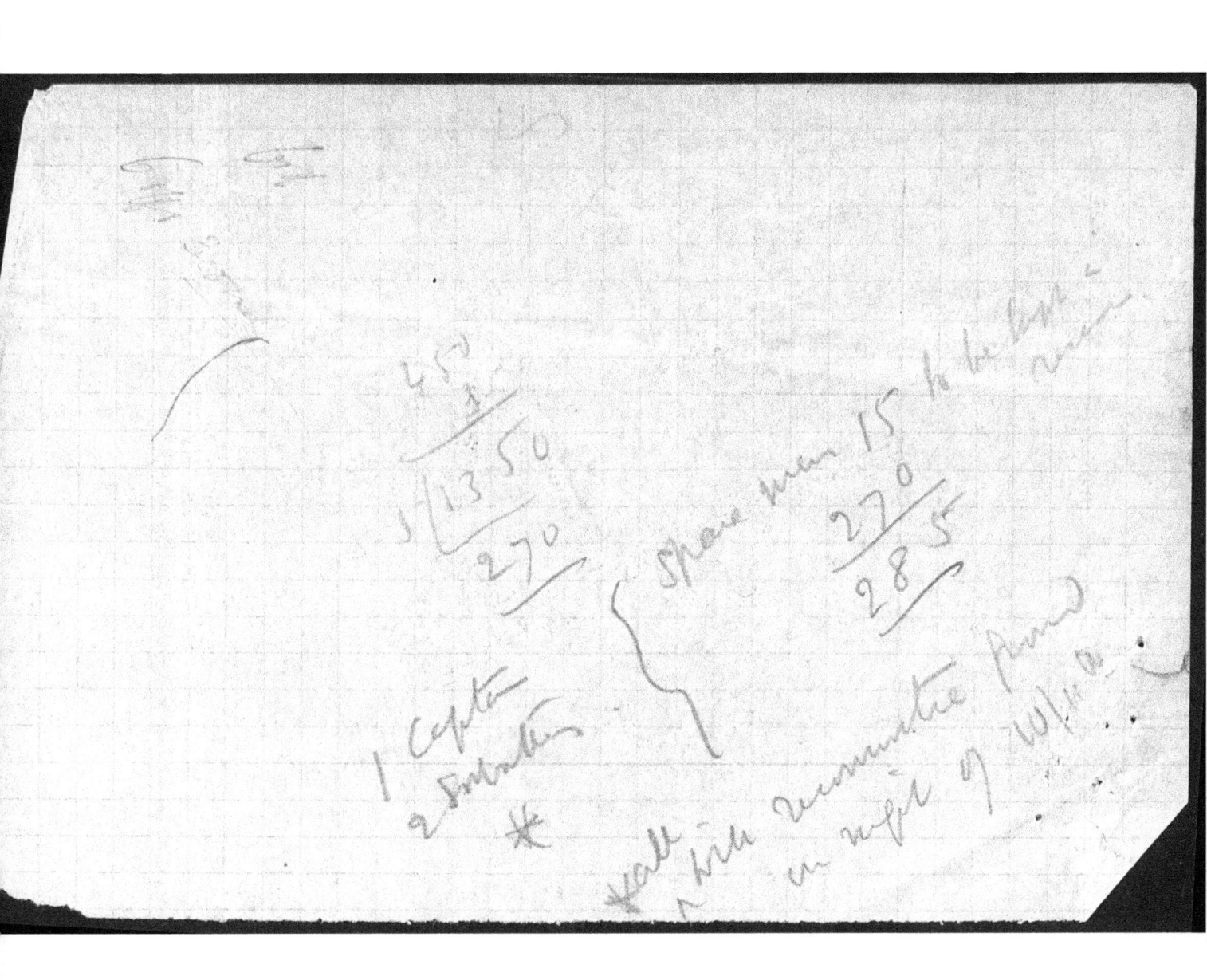

SECRET. Operation Order No 28.   Copy No 6.
by
Lieut Colonel N.A. Thomson D.S.O.
Commdg 8th Seaforth Highlanders   **XXIX**

Ref. 15th Div. Map No 86 d/13/9/16.   16th Sept 1916.

1. "B" & "D" Coys will move to CORPS LINE (East of YORKSHIRE ALLEY) & PEARL ALLEY forthwith.
   All movements to be by platoons at 4 mins interval.
   1st Platoon of "B" Coy to move at once.
   Headquarters will move to THE CUTTING CONTALMAISON immediately after the last platoon of "D" Coy.
   The N.C.O's who reconnoitred the line today, will guide their respective Companies to their new positions.

2. "A" & "C" Coys will remain in their present positions.

3. "B" & "D" Coys will report to Battn Headquarters when they have taken up their new positions.

Distribution No 1. O.C A Coy.   George W. Duncan
              2 " B Coy
              3 " C Coy   Captain
              4 " D Coy   Adjutant 8th Seaforth Highrs
              5. L.G.O.
              6. War Diary
              7. File.

Issued through Signals at 5.50pm.

"A" Form
MESSAGES AND SIGNALS.
Army Form C.212

TO	KS	JB	XXX
	DM		
	ET		

Sender's Number: BM 268
Day of Month: 17
AAA

WARNING ORDER.

With a view to an offensive operation the 44th Inf Bde will take over the line now held by the 45th & 46th Bdes. The 9th Black Watch will probably relieve the 8/10th Gordons on the left line & the 8th Seaforths relieve the 45th I Bde on the right. The 7th Camerons will be in support area roughly LIVER BACON HAM & EGG Trenches. 8/10th Gordons reserve about 6th AV - Lanes KOYLI & HIGHLAND Trenches. Each Battn in line will hold front with 2 coys. The relief will take place night 17/18. Battalions should make necessary reconnaissances today.

From: AR
Place:
Time: 9.25

Those already constructed in M 26 C.

4. Posts will be placed at intervals of 100 yards & will be of the standard plan. They will be occupied by the Battalion which digs them.

5. The Seaforths will construct 5 posts in M 26 d. The 9th Black Watch will construct whatever number of posts may be required in M 26 c to connect up with the existing line.

6. In order to make good THE MILL the trenches to East and West of it must be held and blocked.

7. It is anticipated that determined action by patrols will make them masters of the whole system of trenches without having recourse to a general action.

17/9/16
Issued thro' sigs
9.35 pm.

Kenneth Barge Capt.
B.M. 44. I. B.

NOTE

In accordance with instructions just received operation orders marked A will not be issued.

No op. orders other than those mentioned in B.M. 274 will be undertaken —

Ulsauge
Capt.

17/9/16
9:40 pm

11:20 pm

O.C. "A" & "C" Companies. XXXV D 5/8.

1. The Windmill at M.27.c.1.8 is to be made good & a line of posts is to be constructed along the southern crest of the ridge westwards in M.26.d.f. to join up with those already constructed in M.26.c.

2. Posts will be placed at intervals of 100 yards & will be of the Standard type.
They will be occupied by Coys. in whose immediate front they are situated.

3. Three posts will be constructed opposite the front now held by "A" Coy.
Two posts will be constructed opposite front held by "C" Coy.

4. The 9th Black Watch are to construct whatever number of posts may be required in M.26.c. to connect up with our line of posts.

5. The 5 posts mentioned above will be dug immediately, 3 by "A" Coy & 2 by "C" Coy. Each Coy finding its own covering party.

6. In order to make good the Mill the trenches to the East & West of it must be held & blocked.

7. As soon as construction of posts referred to above is sufficiently far advanced, OC C Coy will send strong patrols to seize & hold trenches in the vicinity of the points mentioned in para 6. & make such other defences as may be necessary.

8. The above operations will be directed by Capt. G. Murray who will ensure co-operation with 50th Div on the right & 9th Black Watch on the left.
He will also keep Battn HQrs informed constantly of the progress being made.

9. Garrisons occupying strong posts must be provided with water, ammunition &c before taking up their positions.

8/9/16.
12.20 A.m.

George W Duncan
Capt & Adj
8/Seaforth Highrs

O.C. "A" Coy.   Information received   XXI D588
                at 6.30 p.m. that message could
                not be read & verbal instructions given.

You will send a strong patrol of 1 Officer &
20 men from the West end of Push Alley
towards the MILL in M.27.E.
They will reconnoitre the ground moving
Northwards & South through M.26.D. & will push
their trench on the Southern side of the Crest
line about M.26.A.7.6. establish a block
facing North & will clear the ground of the
enemy Northwards towards PUSH ALLEY.
The post established by you at about M.26.d.
7.6. will be held & handed over to relieving
unit. The Patrol will be organized by you into
blocking, cleaners & carriers.
You will inform O.C. "C" Coy of your plans & he
will cooperate as you may direct.
You will ring me up on the telephone on
receipt of this & will report whether you wish
a barrage placed on enemy's lines in
M.26. North of pt. M.26.D.7.6. & make any
suggestions you may wish.
This operation will be put in hand at once & you
should endeavour to complete by 7.30 p.m.
by which time the relief should reach
your trenches.
                                    George W Duncan
18/9/16.   for Lt-Col. Cmdg 8th R. Scots.
          (an officer
Sent by hand of 9/7 who left
                at 3-45 p.m.)

"C" Form (Original).
MESSAGES AND SIGNALS.

Army Form C. 2123.
(In books of 50's in duplicate.)

No. of Message ....

| Prefix: SM | Code: OIPP | Words: 83 | Received From: AR | Sent, or sent out | Office Stamp |

Charges to collect .... By: Clifford

Service Instructions: AR

Handed in at: AR   Office: 4.55 a.m.   Received: 5.10 a.m.

TO: DM

| Sender's Number | Day of Month | In reply to Number | AAA |
| G 117 | 17 | | |

Following report from battery commander LV who made personal reconnaissance AAA (1) No signs of enemy in m 26 AAA (2) Trench shown as wired in M 27 a (edition 3 A 1/20000 5 Y C SW) is now non existent and no signs of enemy in m 27 (3) No wire at all in m 26 a b or c AAA (4) Brought in 2 prisoners 229ᵍ R Regt who stated that except for a few snipers there are no germans front of FLERS LINE AAA

FROM
PLACE & TIME: AR

The 9th Black Watch
8th Seaforths —   BM 274
              XXXIV

1. The proposed operation against the hostile trenches in squares M 27 a&c and M 26 a&b will only take place provided the division on our left succeeds in occupying the trenches which it is now attacking.
Certain operation orders are being issued marked "A". These will only be put into execution on ~~the~~ ~~~~ the receipt of further orders from this office.

2. The instructions in the ~~and~~ succeeding paragraphs are to be carried out at once whether or not the orders marked "A" are proceeded with.

3. The WINDMILL M 27 C 18 is to be made good and a line of posts is to be constructed along the southern crest of the ridge westwards to join up with

SECRET

Operation Order No 31   Copy No 8.
by Lt Col M A Thomson DSO
Comdg 5 Seaforth Highlrs.
19 Sept 1916

Reference, ALBERT Combined Sheet 1/40000.

1. The Batt. will march to-day to LAVIEVILLE as follows:
Starting Point:- BECOURT - ALBERT Rd. S.W
Corner of Camp.
Time :- 11-10 a.m.
Order of March :- A.B.C.D. Coys.
All movement East of ALBERT will be by platoon
at 200 yards interval.
On arriving at R.E.3.b.3.1. the leading
Platoon will halt & the remainder will close up.

2. Cookers wagons, Carts will follow the Batt.
The rest of 1st line transport will be Brigaded.

3. Officers valises & mens kit will be dumped under
Coy arrangements in Camp at 10.0.a.m.

4. Particular attention must be paid to March
Discipline.
Platoon Commanders will march in rear of platoons.

5. Special instructions will be issued regarding
tools, bombs, etc.

George W Drum Capt.
Adjt 5 Seaforth Highlrs

Issued through Signals
at 8.45 AM.

Copy No 1. O.C. A Coy   No 6 - Transport Officer
Copy No 2   B   7. Quartermaster
"   3   C   8. War Diary
     4   D   9. File.
     5   L Gun

D/535.

O.C. All Companies.;
Lewis Gun Officer.
Pioneer Officer.
44th I.B.(for information)

1. Training to-morrow will be as follows:-
   From 9a.m. - 1p.m.: Platoon training. Special attention will be paid to Rapid loading, and unloading handling of arms, Fire orders, description of targets, and training of bombing squads.
   The following areas are allotted to Companies:-
   "A".Coy. C.23.a.
   "B".Coy. C.23.b.
   "C".Coy. C.23.c.
   "D".Coy. C.23.d.
   Above refer to Sheet 62 D.First Edition which can be seen in the Orderly Room.

2. All N.C.O's and Men with less than 6 months service will parade outside Battalion Headquarters at 8-45 a.m. to-morrow under the Regimental Sergeant-Major.

3. All Lewis Gunners will carry on training under the Lewis Gun Officer.

4. Pioneers will train under the Pioneer Officer.

5. The assault course is allotted to-morrow as follows:-
   "A".Coy.-3-45p.m. to 4-30p.m.
   "B".Coy.-4-30p.m. to 5-30p.m.
   The exact location of the assault course will be notified later

In the Field,
21-9-16.

........George W. Duncan........Capt. & Adjt,
8th (ser) Battalion Seaforth High'rs.

U R G E N T.   D.596.

O.C.All Coys.
Lewis Gun Officer.
Pioneer Officer.
Quartermaster(for information)

---

1. The Baths situated at PUMP STREET are allotted to-morrow as follows:-

    "A" Company. 7-30.A.M.-9-15.A.M.
    "B" Company. 9-15.A.M.-11.A.M.
    "C" Company. 11.A.M. -12-45.P.M.
    "D" Company. 12-45.P.M.-2-30.P.M.
   Transport,Pioneers,Signallers,
   Pipers & Drummers.   2-30.P.M.-4.P.M.
   About 100 men can bath per hour.

2. The Quartermaster will arrange for a clean supply of Shirts and Socks.

3. Companies will arrange to carry on Training as detailed in this office D.595 of to-day at the same time ensuing that full use is made of the Baths.

4. Reference this Office D.595 re Training to-morrow- Pars 2. These men will now parade at 2-45.P.M.under the Regimental Sergeant Major and not at 8-45.A.M.as therein stated.
   Dress - Skeleton Equipment.

5. Para.5.is now cancelled.

6. 2/Lieut. R.A.Berry-Hart & 2 N.C.O's per Coy will parade outside Battalion Headquarters at 8-30.A.M.to-morrow & proceed to Field Ambulance at pt.C.29.c.o.3.for instruction in Bayonet Fighting under an Instructor of Army Gymnastic Staff.   Instruction will be from 9.A.M.to 12.noon and 2.P.M.to 4.P.M.
   The Officer & N.C.O's will carry rifles,bayonets & scabbards. The N.C.O's should be carefully selected as they will carry out instruction in their respective Coy's at a future date.

In the Field.
21-9-1916.

............George W Duncan............Captain.
Adjutant.8th Bn.Seaforth Highlanders.

D.595/1.

O.C. All Coys.
Lewis Gun Officer.
Pioneer Officer.

1. Training to-morrow will be as follows:-
   From 9.A.M. to 1.P.M.-Platoon & Specialist
   Training as for to-day.

2. All N.C.O's & men with less than 6 months service will parade outside Battalion Headquarters at 8-45.A.M. under the Regimental Sergeant Major.

3. Companies will have their own Lewis Guns to-morrow and will arrange for instruction in the Lewis Gun to be carried on a platoon at a time. This instruction will be under the general supervision of the Lewis Gun Officer-every hour, commencing at 9.A.M. Each Company will send 10 men for instruction under the Lewis Gun Officer in the German Machine Gun.

4. Poineers will train under the Pioneer Officer.

5. The Assult Course is allotted to-morrow as follows:-
   "A"Coy.....3-45.P.M. to 4-30.P.M.
   "B"Coy.....4-30.P.M. to 5-30.P.M.
   2/Lieut.R.A.Berry-Hart & the 8.N.C.O's instructors who attended the Bayonet Fighting Class to-day, will attend at the above hours to assist Companies.
   The exact lacation of the Assult Course willbe notified later.

6. Companies will train on the same ground as to-day.

In the Field.
22-9-1916.
....Captain.
Adjutant.8th Bn.Seaforth Highlanders.

D.595/4.

O.C.All Coys.
Lewis Gun Officer.
Pioneer Officer.
Quartermaster(for information)

XLII

1. Training to-morrow, from 9.A.M. to 1.P.M. will be as follows:-

   (a) The Rifle Ranges at C.24.b & d are allotted as follows:-
       No.1.Range.........."A"Coy.
           2.Range.........."B"Coy.
           3.Range.........."C"Coy.
           4.Range.........."D"Coy.
       1 platoon at a time, per Company will be employed on Musketry.
       Every man will fire two practices -
           1 Deliberate practice of 5 rounds.
           1 Rapid Practice of 10 rounds.
   (b) The remaining platoons of Companies will carry out platoon
       training as on previous two days.
   (c) Special attention should now be paid to the training of
       bombers to complete 32 per Company.
       Each Company will draw 2 Boxes of dummy Mills Bombs from
       the Quartermaster Stores for practice throwing.
       One Officer per Company should be detailed to train
       Company Bombers.

2. All Lewis Gun teams & Lewis Guns will parade under the
   Lewis Gun Officer to-morrow.
   The four ranges mentioned in para 1(a), are allotted to
   Lewis Gun Detachments from 2-30.P.M. to 5.P.M.

3. The Lewis Gun Officer will arrange for "A" Company to have
   the use the Barr & Stroud range finder to-morrow for the
   purpose of checking ranges etc.

4. Pioneers will train under the Pioneer Officer.
5. Stretcher Bearers will parade under the Medical Officer.
6. Not more than 8 men per Company are to be excused parade.
   These should include 4 Company Cooks, 2 Officers Mess
   Servants & Coy Quartermaster Sergeants.
   O.C.Companies will ensure that this order is strictly
   adhered to.

In the Field.
24-9-1916.
                                    George W. Duncan.
                            ....Captain.
                            Adjutant. 8th Bn. Seaforth Highlanders.

D.595/5.

O.C. All Coys.
Lewis Gun Officer.
Pioneer Officer.

1. Training to-morrow will be as follows:-
(a) From 7.A.M. to 8.A.M.
Physical Training.- This will be a muster parade & all specialists (except transport) will parade with their Companies.
All Officers will attend.
Dress:- Clean fatigue dress.
ALL N.C.O's except Coy Sergt Majors & Coy Qr Mr Sergts will parade at 6-50.A.M. outside Bn.H.Q. under the Regimental Sergeant-Major.
Dress:- Rifles, Belts & Sidearms.

(b) From 9-15.A.M. to 1.P.M.
Platoon Training.- Special attention being paid to training of Bombers, Fire Orders, Description of Targets, Handling of Arms etc. Each platoon will have one hours Bayonet Fighting under the Company N.C.O instructors.

All Lewis Gun Teams & Lewis Guns will train under the Lewis Gun Officers.

Pioneers will train under the Pioneer Officer.

The Lewis Gun Officers will arrange for "B" Coy to have the use of the Barr & Stroud Range Finder to-morrow.

In the Field. George W. Duncan
25-9-1916.   ....Captain.
Adjutant. 8th Bn. Seaforth Highdrs.

D.595/6.

O.C. All Coys.
Lewis Gun Officer.
Transport Officer.
Pioneer Officer.

XLIV

1. The Battalion will Route March to-morrow as follows:-

    Starting point - N.E. of FRANVILLERS. (exit)
    Time.   - 9-30.A.M.
    Order of March.- "C" "D" "A" "B" Coys.

    DRESS.   - Marching Order, less Packs, Shrapnel
                     Helmets, Greatcoats & Khaki Aprons.

2. All Lewis Guns will be parked behind Battalion H.Qrs and left under Battalion H.Qr Guard.
   Lewis Gun Teams will parade with their Companies.

3. Cookers & Water Carts will accompany the Battalion. Dinners will be served on the march.
   The Mess Cart will call at Officers Messes at 9.A.M. for any Mess Kit which Officers may wish to take for lunch.

4. Pioneers will parade with their Companies.

5. One man will be left in charge of each billet.

In the Field.
26-9-1916.

George W. Duncan
...................Captain.
Adjutant, 8th Bn. Seaforth Highlanders.

O.C.All Coys.
Lewis Gun Officer.
Pioneer Officer.

D.595/7.

XLV

1. Training to-morrow from 9.A.M.to 1.P.M.will be as follows:-

   (a) The 4 Rifle Ranges at C.24.b & d are allotted && to Coys as before.
   1 platoon at a time per Coy will be employed on Musketry.
   Every man will fire two practices:-
   1 Deliberate of 5 rounds.
   1 Rapid practice of 10 rounds.
   Special attention should be paid to rapid loading and unloading.
   The Pioneer Officer will arrage for targets.

   (b) The remaining Platoons will carry on platoon training as before,including,bayonet fighting,throwing dummy bombs etc.

2. All Lewis Gunners will train under the Lewis Gun Officers. The rifle ranges are allotted to Lewis Gun Detachments during the afternoon.

3. The Lewis Gun Officers will arrange with D Company to have the Barr & Stroud range finder and A Company to have the use of the German Machine Gun to-morrow.

4. Pioneers will carry on training as usual.

5. 2 selected men per Company will report to 2/Lt.J.H.Ross at 9.A.M.to-morrow for instructions as Scouts & Observers. These men should have good eyesight,and if possible have a slight knowledge of Map reading.

In the Field.
27-9-1916.

..............................Captain.
Adjutant.8th Bn.Seaforth Highlanders.

XLVI

D 6 02.

O.C.All Coys.

The following personel will attend a lecture on the New Box Respirator, which is shortly to be taken into use, to-morrow at Divisional Gas School No.5. Billet MONTIGNY at 2-30.P.M.

    1.Officer.   )
    1.Company Sergeant Major.) per Company.
    1.Platoon Sergeant.   )

    Medical Officers Orderly.

The above party will parade outside Bn.H.Qrs at 1.P.M. and march to MONTIGNY under the senior Officer.

In the Field.
27-9-1916.
                    George W. Duncan
                               Captain.
       Adjutant.8th Bn.Seaforth Highlanders.

<u>U R G E N T.</u>

O.C. All Coys.

A/13.
XLVII

1. The following party of 50.O.R. will proceed to ALBERT to-morrow as a permanent working party under C.R.E. 111 Corps.

   "A" Coy.....1.Cpl. & 11 men.
   "B" Coy.....1.L/c. & 13 men.
   "C" Coy.....1.L/c. & 11 men.
   "D" Coy.....1.Sgt. & 11 men.

2. Party will parade outside Bn.H.Qrs at 1-15.P.M Dress:- Full Marching Order - the unconsumed portion of the days ration will be carried on the men.

3. On no account is this to be considered as a punishment or a fatigue, but if possible, the men selected should be those left out of the trenches last time.

4. An advanced party consisting of the 3 N.C.O's detailed by "A" "B" & "C" Coy will parade at Bn.H.Qrs at 8-30.A.M. to-morrow in full marching order where full instructions will be given them.

28-9-1916.   ....Captain.
                 Adjutant. 8th Bn. Seaforth Highlanders.

U R G E N T.

O.C.All Coys.
Quartermaster.

A/13/1.

XLVIII

permanent

1. The following Working Party will be found as under:-

   "A"Coy..........3 men.
   "B"Coy..........1 Lce.Cpl & 3 men.
   "C"Coy..........4 men.
   "D"Coy..........3 men.

2. Party will parade at Bn.H.Qrs at 6.A.M. to-morrow.
   Dress-Full Marching Order, One day's rations will be taken.

3. All these men must be complete in every detail before leaving the Battalion.

4. Duration of work is unknown, but will probably continue while the Brigade is in the present position.

29-9-1916.

..........Captain.
Adjutant 8th Bn.Seaforth Highdrs.

O.C.All Coys.
Lewis Gun Officer.
Pioneer Officer.
44th I.Bde(for information)

D.595/9.

1. Training to-morrow will be as follows:-

   (a) From 9.A.M. to 1.P.M.-Company Training, including Company Drill, Extended Order Drill, training of Bombers, instruction in Map Reading & Observation & Bayonet Fighting.
   (b) Company Bombers will parade at 8-30.A.M.& 1-30.P.M. as to-day to continue Refreshers Course at the Brigade Bombing School.

2. All Lewis Gun Detachments with Lewis Guns & Transport complete will parade in the Field behind Bn.H.Qrs under the Lewis Gun Officers for inspection by the Commanding Officer at 9-30.A.M.

3. Pioneers will carry on training as usual.

4. Scouts will train under 2/Lieut.J.H.Ross.

5. Lewis Gun Officer will arrange for 2/Lieut.J.H.Ross to have the use of the Barr & Stroud Range Finder, and for "C"Company to have the use of the other. "B"Company will have the use of the German Machine Gun.

6. Training will be carried out as before in the Fields immediately N.& N.W of FRANVILLERS.

In the Field.
29-9-1916.

........................Captain.
Adjutant.8th Bn.Seaforth Highlanders.

8th(Service)Battalion Seaforth Highlanders.

Casualties for the month of September,1916.

Officers.

Killed........Nil.
Wounded........1. 2/Lieut.E.M.Fraser. 11/9/16.

Other Ranks.

Killed........2., 6/9/16.
              2., 7/9/16.
              3., 9/9/16.
              4., 15/9/16.
              1., 18/9/16.

Total= 12.

Wounded......14. 7/9/16.
             29. 8/9/16.
             11. 9/9/16.
             12.10/9/16.
              2.11/9/16.
              4.15/9/16.
              9.17/9/16.
             14.18/9/16.

Total= 85.

Missing......1. 18/9/16.

Total= 2.

Grand Total.

Officers   Killed. Nil.
           Wounded. 1.
O.R.   Killed. 12.
           Wounded. 85.
           Missing. 1

99.

In the Field.
30-9-1916.   ....Captain.
                            Adjutant.8th Bn.Seaforth Highlanders.

Reinforcements for the month of September, 1916.

OFFICERS.

September, 19th............Captain.G.F.Thornton.
                           2/Lieut.R.V.Cuthbert.
                           2/Lieut.S.M.Ferguson.
                           2/Lieut.W.Blair.

September, 11th............Lieut.A.A.McLachlan.

September, 12th............2/Lieut.J.Moodie.

September, 27th............2/Lieut.A.F.R.Wyse.

Total = 7

Other Ranks.

September, 1st.............80.

September, 8th.............82.

September, 14th............40.

TOTAL = 122.

In the Field.
30-9-1916.
...............George W. Duncan...............Captain.
Adjutant.8th Bn.Seaforth Highlanders.

SECRET.   COPY No. 2

44TH INFANTRY BRIGADE OPERATION ORDER No. 85.

Reference Trench Map
   OVILLERS. 57.D.S.E. 4.   1/10,000   3rd September 1916.
   Edition 2.B.

1. The 44th Infantry Brigade will move into a forward Divisional Reserve Area on 4th September. This movement to be complete by 8 a.m.

2. Units will move to the following destinations :-
   9th Black Watch. Battn. H.Q. and 3 Companies
                      SHELTER WOOD.
                 1 Company PEAKE WOODS.

   8th Seaforth Hrs. SCOTS REDOUBT.

   8/10th Gordon Hrs. THE DINGLE.

   44th M. G. Company.)
   44th T. M. Battery.) LONELY TRENCH, near the DINGLE.

3. Units will move in the order named below via ALBERT - BECOURT - LOZENGE WOOD Road, by platoons at 200 yards interval.

   9th Black Watch to be clear of their present bivouac by 5-30 a.m.

   8th Seaforth Hrs. to be clear of their present bivouac by 6-30 a.m.

        8/10th Gordon Hrs.
        44th M. G. Company, and
        44th T. M. Battery, to time their march so that the head of 8/10th Gordons passes SHAMROCK TREE at 6-30 a.m.

4. Brigade Headquarters and 7th Cameron Hrs. will remain in their present positions.

5. The 44th Infantry Brigade will relieve 46th Infantry Brigade on the 5th September, in the Right Section, under a separate order which will be issued.

                                              E. A. Back, Major,
                                              Brigade Major,
Issued through
   Signals   44th Infantry Brigade.
   2-0 P.M.

Copy No.		
1	9th Black Watch	10 103rd Inf. Bde.
2	8th Seaforth Hrs.	11 Bde. Signal Officer.
3	8/10th Gordon Hrs.	12 Bde. Transport Officer.
4	7th Cameron Hrs.	13 No. 2 Coy. Train.
5	44th M. G. Coy.	14 Supply Officers
6	44th T.M. Battery.	15 Staff Captain.
7	15th Division.	16 War Diary.
8	45th Inf. Bde.	17 File.
9	46th Inf. Bde.	

SECRET.   Copy No. 2

44th Infantry Brigade Operation Order No. 86.

Reference:-   4-9-1916.
  15th Div. Map No.6a.d/2-9-16.
  and OVILLERS 57.D.S.E.4.
  1/10,000. Edition 2.B.

1. The 44th Infantry Brigade will relieve the 46th Infantry Brigade in the Right Section on 5th September in accordance with Table on reverse.

2. All movements are to be by platoons at not less than 100 yards interval.
   It is most important that troops should not crowd together and that no blocks should occur.

3. 9th Black Watch will remain in their present position.

4. The Advanced Brigade Ammunition and Bomb Dump is at QUARRY (Pt.S.9.a.2.0.) and is refilled from "D" Dump at N.W. corner of MAMETZ WOOD.

   Advanced R.E. Dump is at Pt.X.14.b.2.6.

5. All trench stores will be handed over and receipts given. Advanced parties of all companies except those meeting guides at 3 A.M. will be sent forward for this purpose.

6. Completion of reliefs will be reported by wire to Brigade Headquarters.

7. Brigade Headquarters will close at W.29.d.0.7. at 5-30 P.M. and re-open at the same hour at MAMETZ WOOD. Pt.X.24.a.9.8.

                                        F.A. Beck, Major,
Issued Through   Brigade Major,
  Signals.   44th Infantry Brigade.
  7 P.M.

            Copy No. 1. 9th Black Watch.
                     2. 8th Seaforth Hrs.
                     3. 8/10th Gordon Hrs.
                     4. 7th Cameron Hrs.
                     5. 44th M.G.Coy.
                     6. 44th T.M.Battery.
                     7. 15th Division.
                     8. 46th Inf.Bde.
                     9. 103rd Inf.Bde.
                    10. Right Bde.
                    11. 74th Fld.Coy.R.E.
                    12. 47th Div.Arty.
                    13. 15th Div.Arty.
                    14. III Corps H.A.
                    15. Bde.Transport Officer.
                    16. Bde.Supply Officer.
                    17. No.2 Coy.Train.
                    18. Bde.Bombing Officer.
                    19. Bde.Signal Officer.
                    20. Staff Captain.
                    21. 46th Fld.Amb.
                    22. War Diary.
                    23. File.

RELIEF TABLE TO ACCOMPANY 44TH INFANTRY BRIGADE OPERATION ORDER No.86. DATED 4TH SEPTEMBER, 1916.

Relieving Unit. 44th Inf.Bde.	Unit to be relieved. 46th Inf.Bde.	Guides (6 per Coy.) 1 per platoon. 1 per Lewis Gun. PLACE & TIME.	Route for relieving Unit.	Remarks.
1 Coy. 7th Cameron Hrs.	2 Co's 12th H.L.I. SWANSEA TRENCH.	N.W.Corner of MAMETZ WOOD. 3 A.M.	CONTALMAISON – JUTLAND ALLEY.	Distribution. 7th Camerons. 1 Coy. SWANSEA TRENCH.
1 platoon.	½ Coy. 12th H.L.I. INTERMEDIATE TRENCH.	– do – 3 A.M.	As above.	1 platoon, INTERMEDIATE TRENCH. 2 platoons MILL STREET. 1 platoon in trenches in vicinity of Left Battn. H.Qrs.
3 platoons	1½ (Rear) Co's 12th H.L.I.	– do – 7 A.M.	As convenient.	
1 Coy.	2 (Rear) Co's. 10th Sco:Rifles.	– do – for two leading platoons to ARGYLL ALLEY. 3 P.M. For 2 remaining platoons to CHESTER STR. 1-30 P.M.	Via CONTALMAISON – KENDALL ALLEY.	2 platoons ARGYLL ALLEY. 2 platoons CHESTER STR.
1 Coy.	2 (Front) Co's. 10th Sco: Rifles.	N.W.Corner of MAMETZ WOOD. 6-45 P.M.	Via CONTALMAISON, JUTLAND ALLEY and CLARKES TRENCH.	3 platoons BETHELL SAP. 1 platoon CLARKES TRENCH.
8th Seaforth Hrs.	3 Co's 10/11th H.L.I. 1 Coy. 7/8th K.O.S.B. O.C.1.(Bde.Support).	As above. 10 A.M.	CONTALMAISON.	8th Seaforths will relieve 1 platoon at W.side and 4 Lewis guns at N.W.Corner respectively, of BAZENTIN-le-PETIT WOOD.
8/10th Gordon Hrs.	3 Co's 7/8th K.O.S.B. QUADRANGLE. (Bde. Reserve).	ROUND WOOD. 12 NOON.	Most convenient.	
44th T.M.Battery.	46th T.M.Battery.	On early morning of 5th under arrangements to be made between Officers Commanding concerned.		Mortars and Vickers guns for front line of Right Sub-section to enter JUTLAND ALLEY at 3-30 A.M. on 5th.
44th M.G.Coy.	46th M.G.Coy.			

SECRET.   44th Brigade B.M.124.

All Units 44th Inf.Bde.
H.Q. 15th Division.   For information.

1. The front at present held by the 7th Cameron Hrs. will be sub-divided into two sub-sections, each held by a battalion. The 7th Cameron Hrs. to close to their left and the 9th Black Watch to take over the Right Sub-section.

2. The dividing line between the two sub-sections will be KERRY ALLEY (inclusive to Right Sub-section).
     CARDIFF TRENCH.
     JUTLAND TRENCH inclusive to Left Sub-section.
     MILLS STREET   inclusive to Left Sub-section.
   Note. JUTLAND ALLEY, as a communication trench, can be used by both sub-sections.

3. The relief of the Right front will be carried out to-morrow night, 6/7th; that of back areas, where possible by day to-morrow, 6th, under arrangements to be made between Officers Commanding battalions concerned.

   Accommodation existing, or capable of improvement, is given below as a guide, but it must be clearly understood that where accommodation does not exist it must be made.

4. Existing accommodation in Right Sub-section is -
     BETHELL TRENCH.)
     CLARKS TRENCH.) 1 Coy.
     ARGYLL ALLEY.   1 Coy.
     CHESTER STREET.   1 Coy.
   Note. Accommodation in above must be improved and increased where necessary.

   Accommodation to be provided for 1 Company in or about
     SUTHERLAND TRENCH.
     The platoons being distributed in depth leading platoon about JUNCTION TRENCH, new cuts being made where necessary.
   Battalion H.Q. S.9.c.6.5.

5. Existing accommodation in Left Sub-section. -
     SWANSEA TRENCH.   1 Coy.
     INTERMEDIATE LINE.   )
     A new trench re-dug in front.   ) Half-Coy.

     6TH AVENUE.   )
     A new trench to be re-dug in   ) Half-Coy.
         rear if necessary.   )

     MILL STREET.   )
     Accommodation to be improved   )
         & extended if necessary.   ) 1 Coy.
     (WINDMILL to be avoided.)   )

     Trench running N.W. from   )
         Left Bn. H.Q.   ) 1 platoon.

     Trench running S.W. from   )
         Left Bn.H.Q.   ) 1 platoon.

     Southern end of BAZENTIN-   )
         le-PETIT.   ) 2 platoons.

                                          Major, Brigade Major,
5-9-16.   44th Infantry Brigade.

"A" Form.
MESSAGES AND SIGNALS.

SECRET

TO: NS ET HR
    DH JB KV

Sender's Number: Bm 146
Day of Month: 6

AAA

Warning Order aaa 50th Div will relieve Right Section of 15th Division relief to be complete by noon 10th

From: AR
Time: 10.40 pm

"A" Form. Army Form C. 2121.
MESSAGES AND SIGNALS.

SECRET
S.D.R.

TO { EB
     DM

Sender's Number: BM 136
Day of Month: 6
AAA

Reference BM 133 attached
relief therein mentioned for night
7/8th Sept will be carried
out under arrangements to be
made between O.C. Batt^{ns}
concerned aaa completion of reliefs
to be reported by wire
to Bde. H.Q^{rs}

From: AR
Time: 5.5 p.m.

(Z) EaB.

SECRET.   Copy No. 2

44th Infantry Brigade Operation Order No.87.

Reference :-   7-9-16.
   III Corps Map 1/10,000.
   Sheet 13A. d/4-9-16.

1. On the 8th September the 8/10th Gordon Hrs. will relieve -
   (a) Portion of Seaforth Hrs. now in SWANSEA TRENCH
       between JUTLAND ALLEY (exclusive) and road running
       through S.2.b.& d.

   (b) 24th North: Fusrs. (103rd Inf.Bde.) from just West of
       road running through S.2.b.& d. to Pt.S.2.a.4.2.
       (first sap forward from SANDERSON TRENCH, West of
       BOTTOM ROAD inclusive).

   Relief (a) will be carried out as follows :-
       2 platoons (less 1 fighting ten) 8/10th Gordon Hrs.
       will be working at the clearing of JUNCTION TRENCH
       during the night. A guide 9th Black Watch will meet
       them at junction of JUNCTION TRENCH with WATERS TRENCH
       at 4 A.M. on the 8th and lead them to junction of
       SOMME ALLEY with INTERMEDIATE TRENCH, thence to
       junction SOMME ALLEY with SWANSEA TRENCH.

   Relief (b) will be carried out under arrangements to be
       made between Officers Commanding the Battalions
       concerned.

2. The boundaries of the section taken over by the 8/10th
    Gordon Hrs. will be as follows :-
    Right Boundary.
        A line from Pt.S.2.b.9½.1. to junction INTERMEDIATE
        TRENCH with SOMME ALLEY; thence along Western side of
        SOMME ALLEY.
    Left Boundary.
        A line through Pt.S.2.a.4.2. running South of SANDERSON
        TRENCH to junction WELCH ALLEY with SANDERSON TRENCH,
        along WELCH ALLEY (inclusive to Left Brigade but to be
        used by both) - YORKSHIRE ALLEY (inclusive to Left
        Brigade) - Road junction in X.17.a.Central "Cutting" to
        Right Brigade) - eastern edge of CONTALMAISON PEAKE WOODS
        - main road to ROUND WOOD (exclusive).

3. Battn. H.Q.8/10th Gordon Hrs.- VILLA WOOD. Pt.X.12.c.5.7.

4. O.C.44th M.G.Coy. will relieve 1 Vickers gun of 103rd
    M.G.Coy. on BOTTOM ROAD at S.2.a.5.2½.

    O.C.44th L.T.M.Battery will relieve 1 Stokes gun of 103rd
    L.T.M.Battery in SWANSEA TRENCH at S.2.a.8.2.

5. Completion of reliefs to be reported by wire to Bde.H.Qrs.

                                          E.A.Beck. Major,
Issued through   Brigade Major,
   Signals.   44th Infantry Brigade.
   3-0 P.M.

Copy No.1. 9th Black Watch.   2. 8th Seaforths.   3. 8/10th Gordons.
       4. 7th Camerons.   5. 44 M.G.Coy.   6. 44th T.M.Bty.
       7. 15th Division.   8. 103rd I.B.   9. 15th Div.Arty.
      10. 44th Bde.Signals.   11. Staff Capt.   12. War Diary.
      13. File.   14. 9th Gordons.   15. 45th Brigade.

SECRET.   Copy No. 2

44th Infantry Brigade Operation Order No.88.
_____

Reference 15th Div. Map.   7-9-16.
  Sheets 13A & B. 1/10,000.

1. (a) 1st Division will attack the West portion of HIGH WOOD on
        the 8th instant, their infantry advancing to the assault
        at zero under a barrage which will lift at zero plus
        1½ minutes.

    (b) The 44th Infantry Brigade will co-operate by seizing the
        German trench marked A.B. on accompanying sketch.

    (c) The Southern end of BETHELL SAP will be cleared by Pioneers
        of 50th Division night of 7/8th Sept.

2. 9th Black Watch will carry out this operation advancing under
    the barrage at the same time as the 1st Division. At least
    two companies will be kept available in and near BETHELL SAP
    for this purpose.

3. A "jumping off" trench (C.D.) will be dug by 9th Black Watch
    from Eastern arm of BETHELL SAP to the S.E., parallel with the
    Road and not more than 20 yards from it. Work to be completed
    by 5 A.M. 8-9-16.

4. As soon as the German trench has been occupied it will be
    consolidated and connected to the "jumping off" trench.
    The connecting trench will be so sited as to be defiladed from
    German front line about S.3.b.2.8.

5. 15th Div. Medium T.Ms. (2 guns) and 44th L.T.M. Battery (2 guns)
    will co-operate as follows :-
        15th Div. Medium T.Ms. 1 gun to deal with suspected M.G.
        about S.3.b.9.2½.   1 gun about S.3.b.8.2.8.

        44th L.T.M. Battery.   Both guns assist in barrage,
        thereafter as occasion demands, with special attention
        to M.Gs.
        Stokes guns will be completed to at least 100 rounds per
        gun.

6. Arrangements for covering, clearing and consolidating parties,
    and for the supply of ammunition, bombs and stores, will be made
    by O.C. 9th Black Watch. The necessary dumps will be made in
    BETHELL SAP and in the strong point at S.3.d.4.9.

7. Brigade Signalling Officer will arrange for a Brigade Visual
    Signalling Post to be established at about S.9.a.9½.2.
    (ARGYLL TRENCH).   O.C. 9th Black Watch will be responsible
    for maintaining communication from the trench with this post.

8. On completion of the operation all men of the 9th Black Watch,
    East of the Divisional Boundary, will be relieved by the 1st
    Division but   none of them should be withdrawn until this
    relief is complete.

                                                         P. T. O.

9. The remaining units of the Brigade will be prepared to carry out any instructions they may receive, at shortest notice.

10. Zero time and arrangements for synchronization of watches will be notified later.

Issued through
Signals.
6-30 P.M.

E. Beck. Major,
Brigade Major,
44th Infantry Brigade.

Copy No. 1. 9th Black Watch.
2. 8th Seaforth Hrs.
3. 8/10th Gordons.
4. 7th Camerons.
5. 44th M.G.Coy.
6. 44th T.M.Battery.
7. 15th Division.
8. Brigade Signal Secn:
9. 103rd Inf.Bde.
10. 3rd Inf.Bde.
11. 15th Div.Arty.
12. Div.T.M.Officer.
13. 74th Fld.Coy.R.E.
14. Staff Captain.
15. War Diary.
16. File.

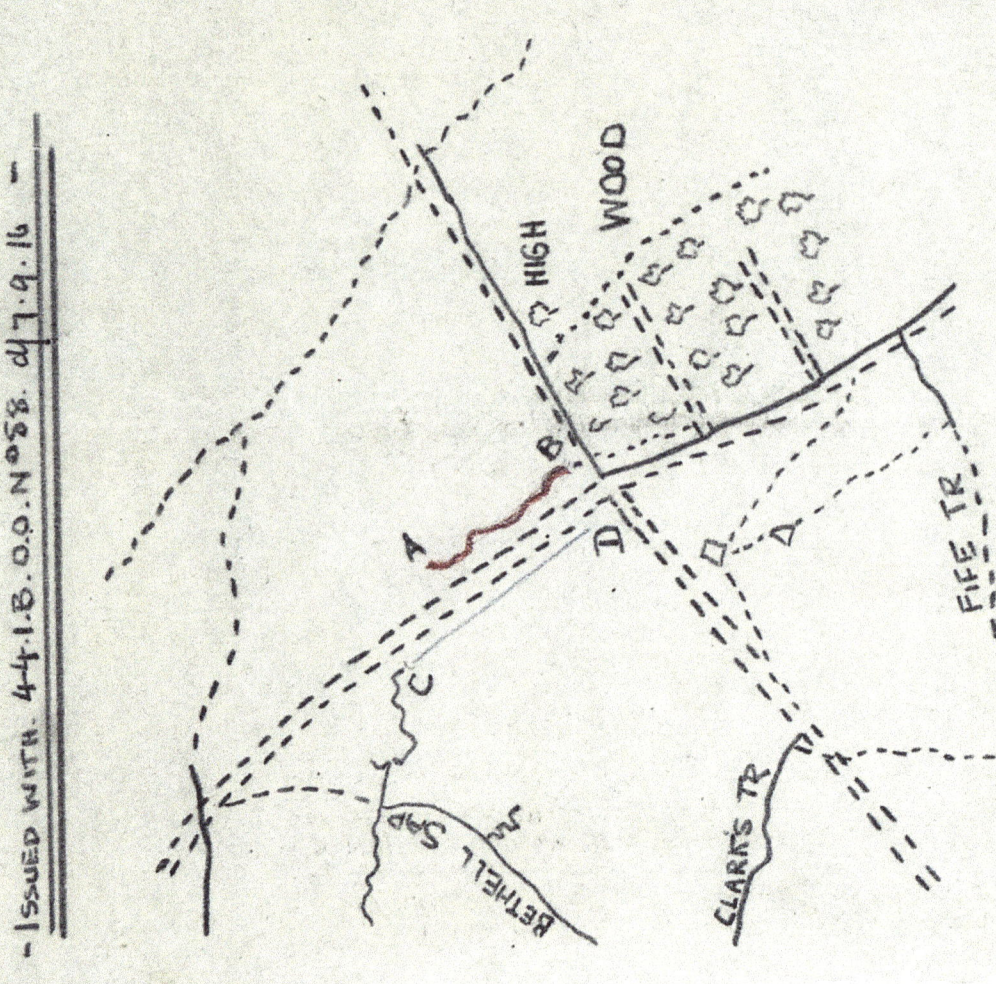

"A" Form. Army Form C. 2121.
MESSAGES AND SIGNALS. No. of Message

TO { K.S.
     D.M.
     E.T. }

Sender's Number: BO. 59
Day of Month: 8/9/16
AAA

Reference B.O. 89 AAA K.S. will draw from Bde. Store 128 bombs AAA. D.M. will use 96 of the bombs they have at HQ AAA. E.T. will draw 96 bombs from Bde. Indymachine? AAA Please arrange two guns placed in position before daylight tomorrow AAA.

From: A.R.
Time: 8 p.m.

SECRET.   Copy No. 2

44th Infantry Brigade Operation Order No.89.

8-9-16.

1. (a) On 9th September, in conjunction with operations
       elsewhere, the 1st Division will be attacking the
       Eastern portion of HIGH WOOD and WOOD LANE.
       In the event of the attack on evening of 8th September
       not being successful, the 1st Division will also be
       attacking the Western portion of HIGH WOOD, and the
       44th Infantry Brigade will again co-operate as on the 8th
       September, should the attack of the 9th Black Watch have
       failed also.

   (b) There will be a deliberate bombardment by Artillery
       beginning at 7 A.M. 9th, and continuing till zero.

   (c) Zero time will be notified later.

2. From zero plus 15 minutes, provided the wind is favourable,
   i.e. South or South-west, the 15th Division will liberate
   smoke along their whole front. This will be done by "P"
   bombs only from the new "jumping off" trench in front of
   CLARKS and SWANSEA Trenches.
   These will be issued, under arrangements to be made by the
   Brigade Bombing Officer, on the following scale.-
   (a) To 9th Black Watch for 400 yards of front, i.e. from head
       of BETHELL SAP to head of KERRY Extension.
   Number of bombs.-
       8 for every 25 yards of front. 8 x 16 = 128.
   (b) To 8/10th Gordon Hrs. for 600 yards of front - Left of
       9th Black Watch Westwards.
   Number of bombs.
       8 for every 25 yards of front. 8 x 24 = 192.
   Note. 1 "P" bomb to be thrown every 2 minutes for 15 minutes.

3. In the event of wind being unfavourable code word "SCOTS" will
   be sent at zero minus 1 hour to units concerned - denoting that
   smoke will not be liberated.

4. During the smoke attack, Left Group Divisional Artillery will
   bombard the German trenches S.W. and S. of MARTINPUICH.

5. Representatives of units concerned will synchronise watches at
   Brigade Headquarters at 11 A.M. on 9th instant.

6. Provided that , the 9th Black Watch capture the line A.B. -
   vide map issued with 44th Infantry Brigade Operation Order
   No.88 - and are still in occupation of it, no further action
   on their part will be necessary, except that of bringing fire to
   bear on all approaches to HIGH WOOD from a Northerly and North-
   easterly direction.

7. In the event of trench mentioned in para.6 not being occupied
   by 9th Black Watch a separate Operation Order will be issued.

Issued through   Major,
   Signals.   Brigade Major,
   1 P.M.   44th Infantry Brigade.
Copies to :-
   1. 9th Black Watch.   2. 8th Seaforths.   3. 8/10th Gordons.
   4. 7th Camerons   5. 44th M.G.Coy.   6. 44th T.M.Battery.
   7. 15th Div.   8. Bde.Signal Offcr. 9. 103rd Inf.Bde.
  10. 3rd Inf.Bde.   11. 15th Div.Arty.   12. Div.T.M.Officer.
  13. 74th Fld.Coy.R.E. 14. Bde.Bombing Offcr. 15. Staff Capt.
  16. War Diary.   17. File.

SECRET.   44th Brigade B.M. 19 D

  ... Inf. Bde.
  9th Black Watch.
  8th Seaforth Hrs.
  44th M.G. Coy.
  44th T.M. Battery.
  15th Division.

1.   Owing to the trenches in the vicinity of
BETHELL SAP having been seriously damaged by shell fire
during yesterday's operations it is impossible to
assemble sufficient men in them to warrant an assault this
afternoon. — It is not possible to work in these trenches
in daylight.

2.   I propose to co-operate as follows :-

60-pr T.Ms.
       At zero minus 15 minutes one gun traverse North-
       western edge of HIGH WOOD until plus 30 minutes;
       thereafter act as circumstances may require.

       At zero minus 5 minutes one gun bombard Cutting at
       S.3.a.2.8. with 30 rounds.

Stokes Guns.

       At zero minus 3 minutes, to zero plus 5 minutes,
       intense bombardment of trench A. B.
       Thereafter one gun will bombard German front line
       from S.3.a.9.6. to S.3.a.2.8.

       One gun in readiness to engage any target which may
       present itself.

Four Vickers Machine guns to fire on N.E. area of HIGH
WOOD, and valley and tracks in M.3.4.c.

Three Lewis guns available to engage targets.

3.   Every endeavour will be made by garrison of
BETHELL SAP to join up eastern arm with trench A. B.

                                        Brigadier Gen.,
9-9-16.   Commdg. 44th Infantry Brigade.

SECRET.   Copy No. 2

14th Infantry Brigade Operation Order No.90.
                                                        8-9-16.

1. On night 9/10th September the following reliefs will take place. -

    (a) 5th North: Fusrs. ("A" Battn. 149th Inf.Bde.) will relieve the 9th Black Watch in the Right Sub-section under arrangements to be made between Officers Commanding Battalions concerned.
    JUTLAND ALLEY to be used as "IN" and "OUT" trench, and relief to be completed by 12 MIDNIGHT.

    On relief 9th Black Watch will move back to billets in ALBERT.

    Billeting parties to meet Staff Captain at Town Major's office, No.99, BAPAUME ROAD, ALBERT, at 2-30 P.M. on 9th September.

    (b) 4th Battn. E.Yorks., 150th Inf.Bde. will relieve 8th Seaforth Hrs. in the Centre Sub-section from Base of BETHELL SAP to S.2.b.7.3. under arrangements to be made between Officers Commanding Battalions concerned.

    SOMME ALLEY to be used as an "IN" and "OUT" trench.

    Relief to be completed by 9 A.M. 10th September.

    (c) On completion of this relief the 8th Seaforth Hrs. will relieve "Y" battalion 103rd Inf.Bde. in O.G.1. and O.G.2. under arrangements to be made between Officers Commanding Battalions concerned.

2. All movements to be by platoons at 400 yards interval.

3. Vickers Guns and L.T.Ms. will be relieved under arrangements to be made by Officers Commanding concerned.
    Guns and mortars for front of Right Sub-section to enter JUTLAND ALLEY 1 hour before the leading platoons of 5th North: Fusrs. front companies.

4. Completion of reliefs will be wired to Brigade H.Qrs.

5. On completion of reliefs (a) and (b) Brigade Headquarters will move to SHELTER WOOD, handing over command and H.Qrs. in MAMETZ WOOD to B.G.C. 149th Inf.Bde.

                                    E.A.Beck, Major,
Issued through   Brigade Major,
    Signals.   14th Infantry Brigade.

    3   P.M.

Copies to -
1. 9th Black Watch.   2. 8th Seaforths.   3. 8/10th Gordons.
4. 7th Camerons.   5. 14th M.G.Coy.   6. 14th T.M.Batt.
7. 15th Div.   8. Bde.Signal Offcr.   9. 103rd Inf.Bde.
10. 3rd Inf.Bde.   11. 149th Inf.Bde.   12. 150th Inf.Bde.
13. 4th E.Yorks.   14. 5th N.Fusrs.   15. 15th Div Arty.
16. 74th Fld.Co,R.E.   17. Bde.Bombing Offcr.   18. Staff Capt
19. War Diary.   20. File.

S E C R E T.   Copy No. 2

Correction No.1. to 44th Infantry Brigade Operation Order No.90.

9-9-16.

1. Owing to an alteration to the Divisional Boundary, the dividing line between 50th and 15th Divisions will be junction SANDERSON TRENCH and PIONEER ALLEY (inclusive to 50th Division) - Point S.2.c.1.7. where railway crosses 70th AVENUE - Pt.S.1.d.7.1. (in 6th AVENUE halfway between WELCH and SCOTCH ALLEYS) - Cross Roads in S.7.b.3.2½. - LOWER WOOD (inclusive to 50th Division), thence original Divisional boundary South-westward.

2. In addition to the 8th Seaforths, that portion of the 8/10th Gordon Hrs. in front and support line between JUTLAND ALLEY and PIONEER ALLEY will be relieved by the 4th Battn., E.Yorks. (150th Inf.Bde.)

   Relief to be completed by 9 A.M. 10th September.

   The portion of the 8/10th Gordon Hrs. thus relieved will be carrying out special work allotted to them, on completion of which they will close in to their left until they are West of PIONEER ALLEY.

3. On the morning of the 10th September the 8/10th Gordon Hrs. will move to the West and relieve "W" Battalion (26th North: Fusrs.) 103rd Inf.Bde.

   The relief to be carried out under arrangements to be made between Officers Commanding Battalions concerned, and to commence at 6 A.M.

4. The boundary between the two brigades in the line, of the 15th Division, will be as follows :-

   Point where CONTALMAISON - MARTINPUICH Road crosses
       CAMERON TRENCH (old Switch Elbow).
   Thence road to where it crosses O.G.2.
   Thence to junction of O.G.1. and YORKSHIRE ALLEY.
   (Along YORKSHIRE ALLEY which can be used by both
   Brigades but is inclusive to Left Brigade).

5. The Stokes Gun in SWANSEA TRENCH at Pt.S.2.a.6.1. and Vickers' gun in BOTTOM ROAD at S.2.a.6.1½. will be relieved by 150th L.T.M.Battery and 150th M.G.Company respectively, under arrangements to be made by Officers Commanding concerned.

Issued through
   Signals.
   10 P.M.

P.A.Beck, Major,
Brigade Major,
44th Infantry Brigade.

Copies to :-
   All recipients of Operation Order No.90.

SECRET.  COPY NO. 2

44TH INFANTRY BRIGADE OPERATION ORDER No. 91.

9 - 9 - 1916.

1. On 10th September the following reliefs will take place :-

    6th North: Fusrs. ("B" Battn. 149th Inf. Bde.) and "B" Battn 150th Inf. Bde. will relieve the 7th Camerons on O.G. line South of BAZENTIN LE PETIT WOOD. Arrangements for relief to be made between Officers Commanding Battalions concerned.
    On relief 7th Camerons will move to Area "B" (see attached Map)

    2 Coys in CUTTING, 2 Coys. in PEARL ALLEY and portion of QUADRANGLE within Area "A".

    Headquarters PEAKE WOOD.

    Relief to be completed by 10 a.m.

2. (a). On 11th September the 7th Cameron Hrs will relieve the 8/10th Gordon Hrs. in front line from Pt.S.2.b.8.4. to S.2.a.4.2.(The Right Section of the new front of 15th Division) under arrangements to be made by Officers Commanding Battalions concerned.

    WELCH ALLEY to be used as an "IN" Trench, SCOTCH ALLEY to be used as an "OUT" Trench, and relief to be completed by 7-30 a.m.

    The 8/10th Gordon Hrs. on relief will move into area "E" (see attached Map)

    Headquarters PEAKE WOOD.

   (b) The 9th Black Watch move from billets in ALBERT into Area "D" (see attached Map) as Brigade Support.

    Headquarters SHELTER WOOD.

    Move to be completed by 10 a.m.

3. All movements to be by platoons at 400 yards interval.

4. Completion of relief and arrival in new positions to be reported by wire to Brigade Headquarters.

                                          E.A. Beck, Major,
                                          Brigade Major,
                                          44th Infantry Brigade.

Issued through
  Signals
at 2-30 P.M.

  Copies to :-
  1. 9th Black Watch.   2. 8th Seaforths.   3. 8/10th Gordons.
  4. 7th Cameron Hrs.   5. 44th M. G. Coy.   6. 44th T. M. Battery.
  7. 15th Division.   8. Bde. Signal Off.   9. 103rd Inf. Bde.
  10. 3rd Inf. Bde.   11 149th Inf. Bde.   12 150th Inf. Bde.
  13. 4th E. Yorks.   14. 5th N. Fusrs.   15. 15th Div. Arty.
  16. 71th Fld.Coy, R.E. 17. Bde. Bombing Off.   18. Staff Captain.
  19. War Diary.   20. File.

        NOTE. Maps issued with Copies 1, 2, 3 & 4 only.

SECRET.   DSS6.

O.C. All Companies.
   Lewis Gun Officer.
   Transport Officer.
      Quartermaster.   Warning Order.

1. The Battalion will probably move from present position at 7.15 p.m. tonight.
   "A" & "C" Coys to Cutting Contalmaison
   "B" & "D" Coys to PEARL ALLEY & PEAKE WOOD.
   HQrs   to PEAKE WOOD.
2. Packs & Greatcoats will be stacked by Companies & returned to 1st line Transport.
3. Every man to march off in fighting dress — Carrying 1 pick or shovel, 5 sandbags, 220 rounds S.A.A., 2 Bombs, (Bombers to carry 6 bombs).
4. Advanced parties are proceeding this afternoon under Lieut. J.H. Ross.
5. Water bottles to be filled before marching off.
6. Dixies will be taken forward in limbers to be detailed by the Transport Officer.
7. Operation Orders follow later.

                                George W. Duncan.
                                        Captain
                        Adjutant 8th Battn Seaforth Highrs

14/9/16

Secret   44th Brigade
                  BM. 2/2

All Units 44th I.B.

    Reference 15th Div. Operation Order No. 90 12th Sept., ZERO will be 6-20 AM 15th September.

                Ulsam, Captain
                Brigade Major
14/9/16.   44th Inf. Bde.

"C" Form (Duplicate).   Army Form C. 2123.
MESSAGES AND SIGNALS.   No. of Message

am FCWPM 34   AR Clifford   XXVII

Service Instructions: AR

Handed in at: AR   Office: 18/p.m.   Received: 6.27/pm.

TO: DM

Sender's Number: BM247   Day of Month: 14   In reply to Number: —   AAA

After 6.30 AM 15th inst. all units must be prepared to move at the very shortest notice AAA Arrangements are being made for the supply of 2 days rations to all troops

FROM PLACE & TIME: A R (44th Inf Bde) 6.5 pm

SECRET.   Copy No. 2

44th Infantry Brigade Operation Order No. 94.

Reference Maps.   Brigade Headquarters.
  15th Div.Maps No.8a, No.8b.   17th Sept., 1916.
  d/13-9-16. 1/10,000.

1. The 44th Infantry Brigade will relieve the 45th and 46th Infantry Brigades on the front M.27.c.2½.1. to the road at M.25.d.8.6. on the night 17/18th September in accordance with the relief table on reverse.

2. The 8/10th Gordon Hrs. return to the 44th Infantry Brigade as reserve battalion on relief.

3. The 3" Stokes Mortars of the 45th and 46th Infantry Brigades in the line will be taken over in position.- Guides as per relief table.
   Machine guns and trench mortars to be in position by 6 P.M.

4. The 73rd Field Coy.R.E. (less two sections) will come under 44th Infantry Brigade on completion of relief.

5. All movements from bivouacs will be by platoons at 300 yards interval.

6. As much water should be carried up as possible. No water can be drawn forward of VILLA WOOD.

7. Orders for relief of 8/10th Gordon Hrs. will be given by the 46th Infantry Brigade.

8. Brigade Headquarters SHELTER WOOD will close at 9 P.M. 17th, and open simultaneously at VILLA WOOD.

9. 300 all ranks of 103rd Infantry Brigade will be attached for carrying duties and will be accommodated in O.G.1. on east side of CONTALMAISON - MARTINPUICH Road.

Issued through   [signature] Captain,
  Signals.   Brigade Major,
  3-30 P.M.   44th Infantry Brigade.

Copies to :-
  No.1. 9th Black Watch.   No.14. Bde.Transport Officer.
    2. 8th Seaforth Hrs.   15. Bde. Supply Officer.
    3. 8/10th Gordon Hrs.   16. Bde. Signal Officer.
    4. 7th Cameron Hrs.   17. Bde. Bombing Officer.
    5. 44th M.G.Coy.   18. No.2 Coy.Train.
    6. 44th T.M.Battery.   19. 15th Div.Arty.
    7. 15th Div.   20. 47th Div.Arty.
    8. 45th Inf.Bde.   21. III Corps H.A.
    9. 46th Inf.Bde.   22. 45th Fld.Amb.
   10. 149th Inf.Bde.   23. Staff Capt.
   11. 2nd Canadian Div.   24. War Diary.
   12. 91st Fld.Coy.R.E.   25. File.
   13. 73rd Fld.Coy.R.E.   26. 103rd Inf.Bde.

Relief Table to accompany 11th Infantry Brigade Operation Order No. 91, dated 17-9-16.

Relieving Units in order of relief.	Units being relieved.	Guides.	Time and Place.	Route.	Headquarters, and area to be taken over.
11th M.G.Coy.	15th & 16th M.G.Coys.	1 Guide from 15th M.G.Coy. and from 16th M.G.Coy. at VILLA WOOD at 3 P.M. Remaining M.Gs. to march to the H.Qrs. 15th M.G.Coy., PEARL ALLEY near VILLA WOOD.		Most convenient.	Headquarters near VILLA WOOD.
11th T.M.Battery.	15th & 16th T.M. Batteries.	1 guide from 15th and 16th T.M.Batteries at VILLA WOOD at 3 P.M. Remaining mortars to march direct to H.Qrs. of 15th T.M. Bty., PEARL ALLEY near VILLA WOOD.		- do -	- do -
9th Black Watch. 1 Coy.	7/8th K.O.S.B. 1 Coy.	2 guides per half company at junction GOURLAY TRENCH and "ARTIMPUICH - CONTALMAISON Road & P.M.		By road as far as GOURLAY TRENCH.	Sunken Road, M.31.D.
9th Black Watch. 1 Coy.	Portion 8/10th Gordon Hrs.	2 guides per Coy. ditto.	6-20 P.M.	- do -	Factory Line.
9th Black Watch. 1 Coy.	8/10th Gordon Hrs.		- do -	- do - 6-10 P.M.	GUIPIT TRENCH.
9th Black Watch. 1 Coy.	10/11th H.L.I.		- do -	- do - 7-0 P.M.	From junction PUSH ALLEY with GUIPIT. Road to present 16th Bde. Boundary. Battn. H.Qr. O.G.1. occupied by 10/11th H.L.I. Advd.H.Q.M.32.a.2.2.
8th Seaforth Hrs.	15th Inf. Bde. (In line)	1 guide per platoon and 1 per Battn.H.Q. at junction of WELCH ALLEY and SANDERSON TR. S.1.d.9.9. 2 Support Co's at 6 P.M. (guides from 11th A.& S.H.) 2 Co's for front line 7 P.M. (guides from 6/7th R.S.F.)		WELCH ALLEY.	Front system on right. H.Qrs. ROYLI TRENCH.
7th Cameron Hrs.	6th Cameron Hrs.	1 guide per platoon and 1 Battn. H.Qrs.at junction O.G.1. and WELCH ALLEY at 8 P.M.		Most convenient.	HAM, EGG, POST and SANDERSON TRENCHES, east of Boundary Rd. Battn.H.Q. Corner of WELCH ALLEY and 6TH AVENUE.

SECRET   Operation Order No 30   Copy No. 5.
            by Lieut Col N A Thomson DSO
            Comdg 8th Seaforth Highlanders.
                                18 Sept. 1916

1. The Battn will be relieved this evening by the 9th Yorkshire Regt.
   Companies will be relieved by the corresponding Coys of the 9th Yorks
   Companies of 9th Yorks will arrive in following order B, D, A, C, + will be met by guides (1 per platoon) from Companies of 8th Seaforth Hrs. at VILLA WOOD at 6 P.M.

2. On relief companies will move back to bivouac in W.29.B.
   ROUTE. CONTALMAISON — BECOURT WOOD.
   All movements to be by Platoons at 300 yds interval

3. 2 limbers will be at MIDDLE WOOD at 8·30 pm to transport mens kits etc to the bivouac.

4. All trench stores will be handed over. — Receipts will be forwarded to Battn Hqrs by 12 noon 19th inst.

5. Companies will bring out their 100% picks & shovels.

6. Completion of reliefs will be reported by wire or runner to Battn Headquarters

Issued through S.P.   George W Drew
at 4-70 pm   Captain
                        Adjt 8th Bn Seaforth Highlanders

Copy No 1 OC A Coy
       2 OC B Coy
       3 OC C Coy
       4 OC D Coy
       5 War Diary
       6 File.

SECRET.   Copy No. 2

44th Infantry Brigade Operation Order No.95.
_____

                                                         18-9-16.

Reference Map.-
  ALBERT Combined Sheet 1/40,000.

1. The 69th Infantry Brigade will relieve the 44th
    Infantry Brigade in the left Sector III Corps on the
    18th September in accordance with table on reverse.

2. All movements to be by platoons at 300 yards interval.

3. During relief all troops will keep in the trenches east
    of O.G. line.

4. All trench stores will be collected at convenient places
    and handed over.   Receipts to be sent to the Brigade
    Office by 4 P.M. 19th.

5. Units will bring out their 100% picks and shovels.
    Surplus tools will be handed over as trench stores.

6. The Nos: 1 of each M.G. and T.M. in the line will remain
    until their services can be dispensed with.

7. Battalions 1st Line Transport - with the exception of water-
    carts and cookers - remain in their present position.

8. Completion of relief will be reported by wire to Brigade
    Headquarters which, on completion of relief, will re-open
    at W.29.d.0.7.

                                        [signature]
                                                    Captain,
Issued through   Brigade Major,
  Signals.   44th Infantry Brigade.

  1.50 P.M.

                    Copy No. 1. 9th Black Watch.
                            2. 8th Seaforth Hrs.
                            3. 8/10th Gordon Hrs.
                            4. 7th Cameron Hrs.
                            5. 44th M.G.Coy.
                            6. 44th T.M.Battery.
                            7. H.Q.15th Div.
                            8. 69th Inf.Bde.
                         9. 45th Inf.Bde.
                           10. 46th Inf.Bde.
                           11. 1st Canadian Bde.
                           12. 150th Inf.Bde.
                           13. 73rd Fld.Coy.R.E.
                           14. 15th Div.Arty.
                           15. III Corps H.A.
                           16. 47th Fld.Amb.
                           17. Bde.Transport Officer.
                           18. Bde.Supply Officer.
                           19. Bde.Signal Officer.
                           20. No.2 Coy.Train.
                           21. Staff Captain.
                           22. War Diary.
                           23. File.

Relief Table to accompany 11th Infantry Brigade Operation Order No.95, dated 19-9-16.

Relieving Units in order of relief.	Units being relieved.	GUIDES.	TIME. P.M.	PLACE.	ROUTE.	DESTINATION.
69th M.G.Coy.	11th M.G.Coy.	1 per gun in line.	4-0	VILLA WOOD.	CONTALMAISON - LOZENGE WOOD & BECOURT.	E.5.b.
69th T.M.Bty.	11th T.M.Bty.	1 per mortar in line.	4-0	VILLA WOOD.		E.5.b.
8th Yorks.	7th Camerons.	1 guide per platoon, 1 Battn. H.Q.	5-30	Junction PEARL ALLEY & CUTTING.		E.5.b.
11th W.Yorks.	9th Black Watch.	- do -	6.30	Junction O.G.1. and CONTALMAISON - MARTINPUICH Road.		X.26.b.
10th W.Riding.	8/10th Gordons.	- do -	5-30	- do -		E.5.b.
9th Yorks.	8th Seaforth Hrs.	- do -	6.30	Junction PEARL ALLEY and CUTTING.	CONTALMAISON and LOZENGE WOOD.	X.29.d.

S E C R E T.   Copy No. 2

44th Infantry Brigade Operation Order No.96.

18-9-16.

Reference Map.-
ALBERT Combined Sheet 1/10,000.

1. The 44th Infantry Brigade will march to-morrow, 19th September, to LAVIEVILLE in accordance with the Table on reverse.

2. Troops will march by platoons at 200 yards interval EAST of of ALBERT.

   Distance of 100 yards to be preserved between Battalions on the march WEST of ALBERT.

3. Cookers and water-carts will follow in rear of their battalions.

   Transport to be brigaded and march in rear of the 9th Black Watch.

4. Billeting parties - who will take over tents from the 46th Infantry Brigade - will meet the Staff Captain at the Town Major's office, LAVIEVILLE, at 6-30 A.M.

5. Particular attention must be paid to march discipline.

   Platoon Commanders will march in rear of their platoons.

6. Reports to the head of the column.

   Brigade Headquarters will open on arrival at the MAIRIE, LAVIEVILLE.

Issued through
    Signals.   Captain,
                                              Brigade Major,
                                           44th Infantry Brigade.
   9.45 P.M.

Copy No.1. 9th Black Watch.   10. Town Major, LAVIEVILLE.
      2. 8th Seaforths.   11. 47th Fld.Amb.
      3. 8/10th Gordons.   12. Bde.Transport Offcr.
      4. 7th Cameron Hrs.   13. Bde.Supply Offcr.
      5. M.G.Coy.   14. Bde.Signalling Offcr.
      6. 44th T.M.Bty.   15. No.2 Coy.Train.
      7. 15th Division.   16. Staff Capt.
      8. 46th Inf.Bde.   17. War Diary.
      9. A.P.M.15th Div.   18. File.

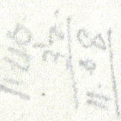

March Table to accompany 11th Infantry Brigade Operation Order No.98.

UNITS, In order of march.	STARTING POINT. Place.	Time.	ROUTE.	DESTINATION.
11th Inf.Bde.H.Q. & Sig.Secn;	SOULT	NOON. 12-0 P.M.	ALBERT - AMIENS	LAVIEVILLE.
8th Seaforth H'rs.	BRIDGE	12-1	Road to Cross	"
7th Cameron H'rs.	on ALBERT	12-11	Roads	"
8/10th Gordons.	- AMIENS	12-21	Pt.D.17.a.0.2.	"
11th M.G.Coy. 11th T.M.Bty.	Road	12-31		"
9th Black Watch.	Point	12-39		"
Brigaded Transport.	E.3.b.3.1.			"

REMARKS. The Brigaded Transport to join column 400 yards in rear of 9th Black Watch. It will be divided into two portions - a distance of 400 yards being maintained between the rear of the transport of the second battalion and the remainder of the Brigaded transport.

S E C R E T.   Copy No. 2

44th Infantry Brigade Operation Order No.97.

19-9-16.

Reference Map.
   AMIENS SHEET 1/100,000.
   ALBERT Combined Sheet 1/40,000.

1. The 44th Infantry Brigade will continue its march to-morrow 20th September, to FRANVILLERS (distance about 8 miles) in accordance with the accompanying March Table.

2. Brigade time will be notified to units between 7-30 and 8 A.M. 20th September.

3. Transport in rear of units.

   Attention is called to previous orders with regard to the position of personnel accompanying transport.

   400 yards distance will be maintained between units.

4. Normal halts will be observed, but if distance has been lost on the march it is to be made good before ~~restarting~~ halting.

5. Billeting parties, on bicycles, will meet Staff Captain at the Town Major's office, FRANVILLERS, 7-30 A.M. 20th September.

6. Reports to the head of column.
   Brigade Headquarters open on arrival at the MAIRIE, FRANVILLERS.

Issued through
   Signals.
   5 P.M.

Captain,
Brigade Major,
44th Infantry Brigade

Copy No. 1. 9th Black Watch.
        2. 8th Seaforths.
        3. 8/10th Gordons.
        4. 7th Camerons.
        5. 44th M.G.Coy.
        6. 44th T.M.Battery.
        7. H.Q.15th Division.
        8. A.P.M. 15th Div.
        9. Town Major, FRANVILLERS.
       10. Bde.Transport Officer.
       11. Bde.Supply Officer.
       12. Bde.Signalling Officer.
       13. No.2 Coy. Train.
       14. 73rd Fld.Coy, R.E.
       15. Staff Captain.
       16. War Diary.
       17. File.

March Table to accompany 44th Infantry Brigade Operation Order No.97.

UNITS, In order of march.	STARTING POINT. Place.	Time.	ROUTE.	DESTINATION.
1 platoon 9th B.Watch.	Cross Roads ALBERT - AMIENS and LAVIEVILLE - RIBEMONT. D.18.a.3.4.	A.M. 10-0	ALBERT - AMIENS	FRANVILLERS.
44th I.B. H.Qrs. and Signal Secn:		10-1	Road to Cross	(Billets and bivouacs).
9th Black Watch. (Less 1 platoon)		10-3	Roads	
8th Seaforth Hrs.		10-13	FRANVILLERS -	
7th Cameron Hrs.		10-23		
8/10th Gordons.		10-33	HEILLY.	
44th M.G.Coy. 44th T.M.Bty.		10-43		
73rd Fld.Coy.R.E.		10-49		

REMARKS.

Care must be taken that the Cross Roads in the village are not blocked.

SECRET   44th Brigade B.M. 23

All Units 44th Infantry Brigade

Information has been received that previous experience shows that it is possible a counter attack in retaliation for our offensive operation today may be launched from the German front line in S.2.b. and S.3.a.

Units should therefore be on the look out for any signs of hostile activity on their front and at once deal with it.

The contact aeroplane which will fly over at 6-30 p.m. 8th inst. should be watched, which will drop Smoke Bombs as an "S.O.S." signal in the event of observing hostile troops massing.

Lewis Guns in advanced positions should be able to deal effectively with any hostile attack coming over the hill.

8th Sept. 1916.

E. A. Beck, Major.
Brigade Major.
44th Infantry Brigade.

- 2 -

D.503.

Officers Commanding.
All Companies.

Above for your information. —

O.C. "B" & "D" Coys will each detail an officer to watch contact aeroplane and report immediately, should the "S.O.S" signal be dropped.

George W. Duncan.
Captain
Adjt. 8th Seaforth Highlanders.

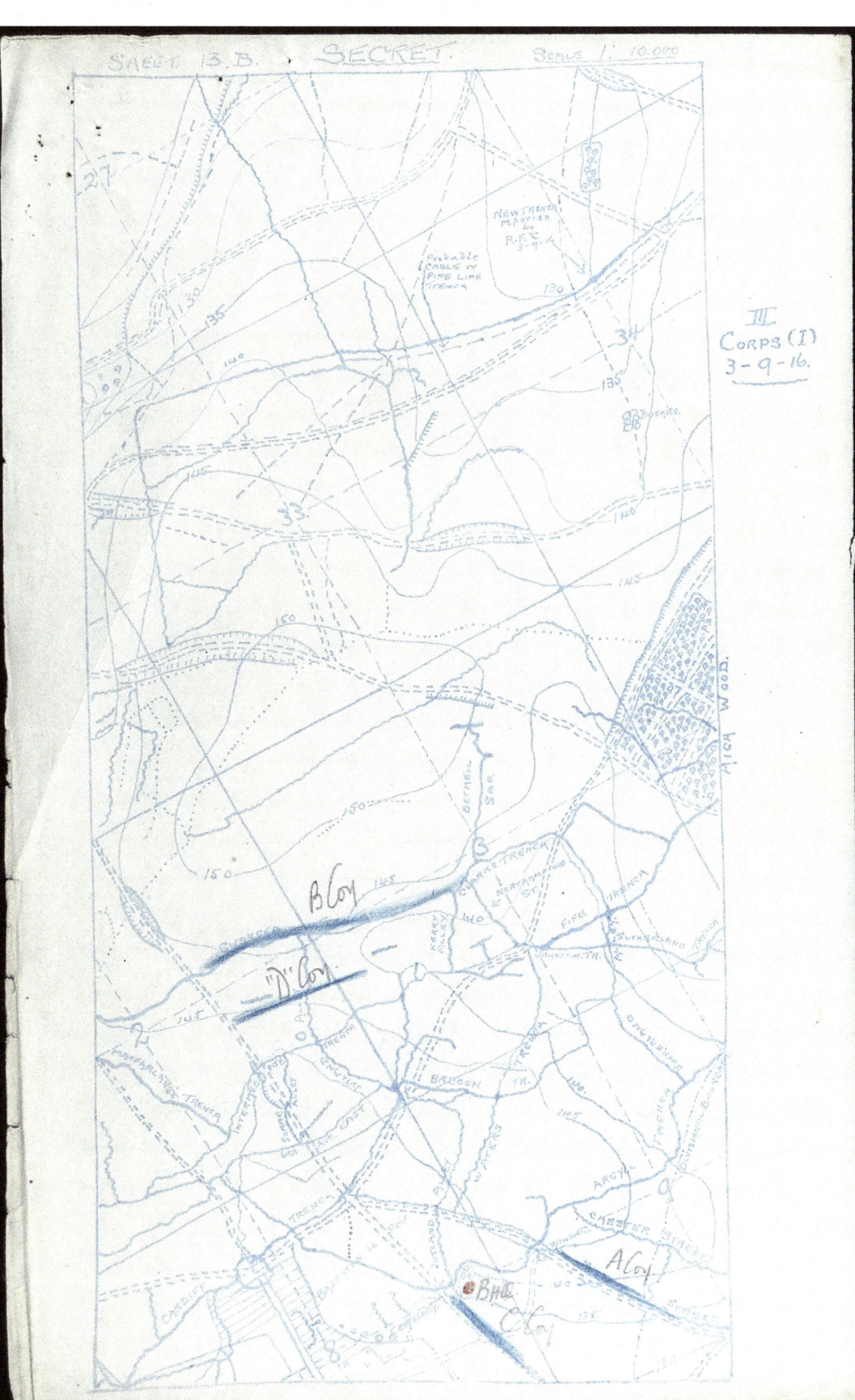

www.ingramcontent.com/pod-product-compliance
Lightning Source LLC
Chambersburg PA
CBHW080851230426
43662CB00013B/2074